LIVING HOPE

Powerful Messages of Faith

by

Pastor Kurt Jacobson

Published by eBookIt.com

http://www.eBookIt.com

ISBN: 978-1-4566-3294-6

Dedicated to

Maridale Valesh Jacobson

My mother
A woman of deep faith and boundless spirit

Contents

Preface

This book is my latest, and likely final effort, to assemble a collection of messages for people who are curious about how much God loves. Throughout the three decades I wrote sermons, I always wanted the Word to inspire those who came to worship. I wanted people to encounter the Upper Story of God, meaning the big picture—the sweeping narrative of how God seeks to be in a relationship with us. I also wanted to provide insight into how God enters and intersects with our lives, the Lower Story.

I knew every Sunday that there were people thirsting for soul-sustaining hope, grace and guidance. What I want *Living Hope* to provide is another experience of the Upper Story and the personal story. Throughout these thirty years, I've been blessed by thousands of willing listeners who have received something of meaning. After the enthusiastic response to "Welcoming Grace: Words of Love for All," this newest collection was born.

This first section of this book is a collection of sermons. They contain many stories based on biblical passages that draw readers into both the Upper Story and Lower Story of God. The Upper Story continually redeems and renews.

The Lower Story contains the portraits of people, ancient and contemporary: Moses, Samuel, Eli, Vashti, Mary, Joseph, the disciples, the blind man, you and me. Through these personal narratives we see that the actions and predicaments of people are transformed by God's amazing patience, forgiveness, mercy and direction.

I hope you find your life in the Upper Story. We know our own stories well, yet without the connection to a greater good, a crisis or a major loss in life could be seen as an experience without hope. But put into the context of the Upper Story and God's amazing goodness, that crisis or loss can be seen differently, perhaps through which God reveals something life-giving, new or redeeming.

Many of the sermons in *Living Hope* come from the privilege of having a long span of ministry with the fine people of Trinity Lutheran Church in Eau Claire, Wisconsin. Others were shared while serving as an interim pastor, during times of change with the people of First Lutheran Church of Barron, Wisconsin and Our Saviour's Lutheran Church of Chippewa Falls, Wisconsin. The faithful people of these churches inspired me, and I cherish the memories of the time with them.

The last section of this book are entries from my Caring Bridge site. This portion has a very personal dimension. These writings amplify my Lower Story and detail the life-changing news of being diagnosed in March 2018 with advanced non-small cell lung cancer. When I learned of this diagnosis, the cancer had spread through my body and into my brain.

I added this section for two reasons: First, because many people asked if I would publish them. The interest and care of many people has touched me deeply. Secondly, these writing show, from my personal perspective, how the Lower Story is lifted and transformed by the Upper Story.

Writing for Caring Bridge has been more challenging than writing sermons. I have never been a preacher inclined to include stories of myself in sermons. I always tried to keep my Lower Story out of view, instead desiring to allow my listeners to connect with their own Lower Story. However, when I do appear in my sermons, my goal was to show the need to be forgiven or redirected in hopes that my listeners might discover a gracious and patient God! Truth be told, there were far more interesting, intelligent and insightful people to populate sermons.

At the beginning of my lung cancer diagnosis, I set out to use Caring Bridge to manage communication and respond to people's inquiries about my wellbeing. What I quickly discovered was that I could not make the entries only about me. I needed a focus beyond myself and information about diagnoses and treatments. I needed the Upper Story! Thus, what I hope you will find in the second section is the timeless, biblical message of hope, comfort, encouragement and new life. In many ways, the message that I have aspired to share for three decades unfolds like never before.

I could fill several pages with words of thanks and still leave someone out. I thank God for the people who listened to my sermons. I thank Andra Palmer who coordinated all aspects of seeing this book through to publication; Nancy Vrieze, Steven Josephson and Todd Wright who edited the final draft. Finally, thanks to eBookIt.com for their excellent work in publishing and design process.

Section I: *A Collection of Sermons*

A Clear Bias

Luke 6:17-26

He came down with them and stood on a level place, with a great crowd of his disciples and a great multitude of people from all Judea, Jerusalem, and the coast of Tyre and Sidon. They had come to hear him and to be healed of their diseases; and those who were troubled with unclean spirits were cured. And all in the crowd were trying to touch him, for power came out from him and healed all of them.

Then he looked up at his disciples and said:

'Blessed are you who are poor, for yours is the kingdom of God.

'Blessed are you who are hungry now, for you will be filled.

'Blessed are you who weep now, for you will laugh.

'Blessed are you when people hate you, and when they exclude you, revile you, and defame you on account of the Son of Man. Rejoice on that day and leap for joy, for surely your reward is great in heaven; for that is what their ancestors did to the prophets.

'But woe to you who are rich, for you have received your consolation.

'Woe to you who are full now, for you will be hungry.

'Woe to you who are laughing now, for you will mourn and weep.

'Woe to you when all speak well of you, for that is what their ancestors did to the false prophets.

Dear Sisters and Brothers, may the grace and peace of God in Christ be yours in abundance this day, and always. Amen.

In a Peanuts comic strip one day Lucy reports to Charlie Brown saying: "I have examined my life and have found it to be without flaw! Therefore, I'm going to hold a ceremony and present myself with a medal. I will then give a moving acceptance speech. And after that, I'll greet myself in the receiving line." Lucy concludes, "When you're so good, you just have to do everything yourself."

Have you ever known a Lucy? Someone who is so self-confident, so self-reliant? These folks set extremely high expectations for themselves.

As I have pondered and studied today's Bible reading from Luke in the past week, I have thought about expectations. Sometimes we set so many expectations for ourselves. We want to be the best doctor, lawyer, teacher; we want to be the good parent, coach, math student, jazz band member, basketball player.

However, I would guess that we are better at setting expectations for other people. I know that in the years I have been a pastor, I have encountered many expectations people have for me because of my position. People have expected me to know when they are hospitalized, become unemployed, or having marriage difficulties, so that I might offer pastoral care.

In those situations where someone sets expectations of us without communicating them, hard feelings are sure to be the result.

Whatever the expectations we set for ourselves or others, I have a question that I want you to think about as we gather here today to worship God.

What are your expectations of God?

Have you ever thought about that? To me it is an intriguing question: What are my expectations of God? With what agenda do you seek God here today in this gathering?

I've been asking that question of others and the responses have been interesting. What I've heard:

- I expect that God is always going to be there for me.

- I expect that God is going to always love me, no matter what.

- I expect that God is going to give me eternal life.

- I expect that God is going to forgive me and will help me forgive others.

- I expect that God is going to help me do right in my life.

Now, if I was Oprah, I would be hopping on down to you and soliciting your responses. In a way, I would like to do that! However, to save anyone from embarrassment, I will refrain.

In my interviews on expectations of God, I was not surprised. They were all good responses and probably quite representative of American Christians.

What I did not hear is an expectation of God that calls forth anything from us. Well, today's Bible reading does just that very clearly. *I expect that God is going to change me.*

Would you like to hold such an expectation of God? Did you come here this morning hoping that God's Word would change you?

Well, that is the agenda that God has for us today in the Bible reading from Luke. Jesus is blatant in setting an expectation for every one of us. He expects that we who have money, power, and well-functioning lives will work to improve the lives of those who do not. Because Jesus knows that our money, our position and our reputation all too easily become a means by which we think we are self-sufficient. People even think that their wealth and status are blessings from God. If you doubt me, look again at Jesus' words today. He says:

Blessed are you who are poor, hungry or excluded, "for your reward is great in heaven."

Then he said:

> Woe to you who are rich;
> Woe to you who have full stomachs;
> Woe to you who laugh now for the day is coming when you won't be rich, you will be hungry, and you will weep.

Is that challenging enough? To be honest, Jesus' words make me nervous, not happy, and a bit ill-at-ease.

Let's face facts. We live in a very, very privileged society. We are rich people. And we live in a society that rewards those who make their own way. We are told to set our goals high, grab for all we can get to insure our own future. Accumulate your wealth now, so you can be independent in your retirement. It's a get ahead world and it's up to you to get yourself ahead.

But then you come here for this time of worship and you hear the words of Jesus which are totally opposite the ways of the world. Jesus talks about rewarding the poor and hungry and sad. He says the rich, the full, the happy are not blessed. Clearly, God has a bias towards the poor. My friends, we are not the poor. The blessings of God reverse human values we hold dear.

Considering our Midwestern, middle-income lives, I think we could rewrite these words of Jesus and feel better about them. How about this:

Blessed are the pushers, for they get ahead in the world;

Blessed are the hard-boiled, for they never let life hurt them;

Blessed are those who complain, for they get their own way in the world;

Blessed are the slave-drivers, for they get results;

Blessed are the knowledgeable people of the world, for they know their way around;

Blessed are the trouble-makers, for they make people take notice of them.

This approach to life by some people contradicts the way of life designed by God. Jesus' words of woe condemn our human values.

I am the first to admit that Jesus' words of woe hit me hard. We are not poor people by the world's standard of poor. Yes, we are reluctant to admit we are rich. It is so easy to look at others and see their wealth as so much more than ours. If you have traveled beyond this country, you have seen other standards of living, quite unlike the prominent standard we have in the U.S.

In four weeks, a few dozen people from this congregation will be in Jamaica as part of a congregational mission trip where we will be working with the poor of that island. For many in our group, this will be their first time to see whole neighborhoods and cities of people living in squalor. When we leave the Kingston airport en route to our hotel, we will pass through neighborhoods where corrugated steel and scrap lumber form homes for young families. And in that moment, it will be hard, virtually impossible to say: "I'm not a rich person."

Our new missionaries, Tom and Eunice Olson and their three young children live in the Central African Republic. They recently wrote us a letter as they were preparing to return to Africa after a few months here in America. They write:

"The American culture of consumerism is so overwhelming and addictive that it blinds everyone to its toxicity while it snares us in its trap." So,

To us rich people, Jesus says: WOE!

To us well-fed people, Jesus says: WOE!

To us people who are praised and respected by others, Jesus says: WOE!

Why is Jesus saying these things? Is Jesus a big spoil sport? Doesn't the world go around because there are people with money who employ others so that they too can provide for themselves? And isn't a basic aspect of life to be respected and spoken well of?

The "woe" words of Jesus, spelled w-o-e might be more enlightening for us when spelled w-h-o-a, the word used to stop a horse or someone in the hallway. Jesus is giving us a stern warning: "Whoa, slow down, stop for a moment to think about your life and your values." Jesus wants us to remember that we are made to be blessings to other people. Jesus shows us God's bias for the poor, hungry, and sad. So, where does that leave us? How are we to live?

Well, as Christians, well-fed and wealthy by the standard of the world, we must look to Jesus and how he lived giving of himself, spurning worldly values and anything, anything at all that diverted his vision of God's kingdom. Perhaps we must first stop and ask ourselves: Do the values I hold fit with God's ways made known in Jesus? Do the decisions I make about how I live, spend my money and share my time reflect God's love and care to the poor and hungry of this world?

I continue to struggle with Jesus' words, and even my own words today. I have wrestled with them all week.

Finally, I ask myself: Is there any good news for me and you in these words of Jesus today? Surely there is--but to decipher it without first struggling with Jesus' strong teaching about our rich, privileged lives misses the point. I am condemned by Jesus' teaching. The woes are for me and you. I am forced, as disquieting and unpleasant as it may be, to rethink and adjust my life's values.

So where is the good news? The good news is that we have a God who gives us signs in our lives that are intended to redirect our thinking and acting.

I am grateful that God holds expectations for us that call forth from us changes in attitudes and behaviors. It is only through the power of Christ at work in our lives that the present woes of our times can be reversed. When the words of Jesus today become effective, they redirect our values and actions and change our lives, so that we might more clearly reflect the ways of God. That is good news.

A Transition of Royal Proportions

I Samuel 9

There was a man from the tribe of Benjamin named Kish. He was the son of Abiel, grandson of Zeror, great-grandson of Becorath, great-great-grandson of Aphiah - a Benjaminite of stalwart character. He had a son, Saul, a most handsome young man. There was none finer - he literally stood head and shoulders above the crowd! Some of Kish's donkeys got lost. Kish said to his son, "Saul, take one of the servants with you and go look for the donkeys." Saul took one of the servants and went to find the donkeys. They went into the hill country of Ephraim around Shalisha, but didn't find them. Then they went over to Shaalim - no luck. Then to Jabin, and still nothing.

When they got to Zuph, Saul said to the young man with him, "Enough of this. Let's go back. Soon my father is going to forget about the donkeys and start worrying about us." He replied, "Not so fast. There's a holy man in this town. He carries a lot of weight around here. What he says is always right on the mark. Maybe he can tell us where to go." Saul said, "If we go, what do we have to give him? There's no more bread in our sacks. We've nothing to bring as a gift to the holy man. Do we have anything else?" The servant spoke up, "Look, I just happen to have this silver coin! I'll give it to the holy man and he'll tell us how to proceed!" (In former times in Israel, a person who wanted to seek God's word on a matter would say, "Let's visit the Seer," because the one we now call "the Prophet" used to be called "the Seer.") "Good," said Saul, "let's go." And they set off for the town where the holy man lived.

As they were climbing up the hill into the town, they met some girls who were coming out to draw water. They said to them, "Is this where the Seer lives?" They answered, "It sure is - just ahead. Hurry up. He's come today because the people have prepared a sacrifice at the shrine. As soon as you enter the town, you can catch him before he goes up to the shrine to eat. The people won't eat until he arrives, for he has to bless the sacrifice. Only then can everyone eat. So get going. You're sure to find him!"

They continued their climb and entered the city. And then there he was - Samuel! - coming straight toward them on his way to the shrine! The very day before, God had confided in Samuel, "This time tomorrow, I'm sending a man from the land of Benjamin to meet you. You're to anoint him as prince over my people Israel. He will free my people from Philistine oppression. Yes, I know all about their hard circumstances. I've heard their cries for help."

The moment Samuel laid eyes on Saul, God said, "He's the one, the man I told you about. This is the one who will keep my people in check." Saul came up to Samuel in the street and said, "Pardon me, but can you tell me where the Seer lives?" "I'm the Seer," said Samuel. "Accompany me to the shrine and eat with me. In the morning I'll tell you all about what's on your mind and send you on your way. And by the way, your lost donkeys - the ones you've been hunting for the last three days - have been found, so don't worry about them. At this moment, Israel's future is in your hands." Saul answered, "But I'm only a Benjaminite, from the smallest of Israel's tribes, and from the most insignificant clan in the tribe at that. Why are you talking to me like this?"

Samuel took Saul and his servant and led them into the dining hall at the shrine and seated them at the head of the table. There were about thirty guests. Then Samuel directed the chef, "Bring the choice cut I pointed out to you, the one I told you to reserve." The chef brought it and placed it before Saul with a flourish, saying, "This meal was kept aside just for you. Eat! It was especially prepared for this time and occasion with these guests."

Afterward they went down from the shrine into the city. A bed was prepared for Saul on the breeze-cooled roof of Samuel's house. They woke at the break of day. Samuel called to Saul on the roof, "Get up and I'll send you off." Saul got up and the two of them went out in the street. As they approached the outskirts of town, Samuel said to Saul, "Tell your servant to go on ahead of us. You stay with me for a bit. I have a word of God to give you." (The Message)

Editor's Note:

This message and others uses the metaphor of the Upper Story and Lower Story from "The Story" by Randy Frazee and Max Lucado. The Upper Story tells the big picture, the grand narrative of God seeking to be in relationship with humanity as it unfolds throughout history. The Lower Story contains the details of particular people, the episodes we've become familiar with: Adam and Eve, Cain and Abel, the flood, etc.

Dear Sisters and Brothers, grace and peace be with you all:

In 2015 I enjoyed a travel adventure in Israel, Palestine and Jordan with 28 friends and members from the church I served. We enjoyed seeing many Old and New Testament biblical sites. We stood on Mount Nebo in Jordan where Moses is reported to have seen the Promised Land but died before entering it. We waded in the Jordan River and along the shore of the Sea of Galilee. Our trip was a smorgasbord of amazing history, culture and current events.

There is often news coming out of this region telling of conflicts between Israeli and Palestinians, Jews and Muslims. Travel in that region is often out of the question for some people because fear stops them. However, we learned so much through this travel experience, and we found no reason to fear. By the time we departed, we understood that any hope of solution will require a transition of thinking.

Surely, life continues to be in transition for people in East Jerusalem and the West Bank of Palestine. Like so many of the major transitions evident in the stories of the Old Testament, real time transitions are happening in a large way in the biblical lands of the Middle East today. More barriers are going skyward in Israel, walling off people who live in Palestine. They cannot move freely as we do in the USA. The entire Middle East seems to be in a notable state of change. Conflict, unrest, fear and anxiety mark much of the transition underway in that part of the world.

Transitions are always upon us. The design of human life is always under the umbrella of transition. As we age and move through the stages of life, transitions come upon us, ready or not. The better we accept them and understand how to move through them, the better prepared we will be to see that God is with us, guiding us through transitions. We call that kind of activity of God in our lives the Upper Story.

In the biblical story of I Samuel, the people of Israel are demanding a transition. They want a king to lead them. They want a different type of leadership than God has provided in the past. So far, God has provided people like Moses, Aaron, Joshua, and Eli--prophets and priests to lead the people of Israel. Now, in I Samuel, the people are demanding a king.

Samuel, who has grown up under the tutelage of the priest named Eli, comes on the scene when the people of Israel are under threat by the Philistines. With Eli's two corrupt sons leading the army, the people fight one war with the Philistines and they lose. Before fighting a second time, they decide to take God along, a.k.a. the Ark of the Covenant, thinking it a divine rabbit foot to insure their victory. And yet they still lose. Eli's two sons are killed and worse yet, the Philistines capture the Ark! When Eli hears this news, he falls off his chair, breaks his neck and dies. Samuel, as the leader in waiting, now inherits a mess.

Winter had come to the people of Israel. This Lower Story, the story of human life with all its failure and folly, seems bleak. So, it is time to look for the Upper Story of God's actions to bring hope and redemption. But that isn't going to come any time soon.

What happens next is the people rise up, demanding transition. They demand a different type of leadership. They don't want another priest or prophet. They want a king like all their neighboring countries. (*"No! But we are determined to have a king over us, so that we also may be like other nations, and that our king may govern us and go out before us and fight our battles."* (I Samuel 9:19-20)

Do you wonder why they wanted a king? Perhaps the Israelites thought that if they could have a king, then they would be stronger and able to conquer their enemies. But in this Lower story, the people are forgetting all the times God had provided for them in transition. Rather than continue trusting God, they believed that they could do it better, if things were left in their control. The request for a king as leader is a transition in Israel's history which would forever change them, and not for the better.

One of my favorite Broadway productions of recent years is Lion King. In that story, the young cub Simba dreams of the day when he will become king and have the power to control everything. To be in charge and in control is the desire of not just fictional bear cubs, but people, too.

In the Lower Story, the truth is we always want to be in charge. We hold tightly to the freedom we feel is our birthright, to be the boss of our own lives. We want to be kings and queens! But as we'll see, when Samuel appoints a king for the Israelites, God isn't pleased.

After the people shout their desire for a king, Samuel is troubled. He takes this request as a personal affront and challenge to his leadership. So, he seeks God's advice. Essentially, God tells Samuel, "They're not rebelling against you but against me, and they've done it repeatedly since I rescued them from Egypt. Tell them they can have their king, but that it's going to cost them."

It's a bit comical, but mostly sad, isn't it, the price we're willing to pay to be in control. In the Lower Story, all the other nations surrounding Israel have kings, but the Israelites have religious people leading them. Kings could make decisions on the spot. Religious leaders checked in with God first. Kings were hailed as royalty; religious leaders were more often ignored.

But what's even more sad here is that God's desire for these people continues to be stymied by them and their insistence to call their own shots and be in control. The overall goal of the Upper Story, the entire narrative of the Scriptures, is the relentless pursuit of God to be in relationship with these people and it seems to be at a very low point here in I Samuel. Yet, there's something important to see. God changes God's mind and consents to the people's request to have a king. What's the point? Sometimes God gives you want you want, even if it's not what God wants for you. God always prefers that in our Lower Story we do things God's way, not because God must have God's own way, but because God loves. God knows what will make our lives better.

But we don't always do things God's way, which in the end usually makes our lives miserable. So, Samuel appoints for the people their first King, Saul, and he instructs Saul of the importance of obeying God and faithfully serving as one come from God. But you can probably guess what happened during Saul's reign. While he shows good potential at the start, Saul assumes control and quickly forgets everything Samuel said. Throughout Saul's reign, the Israelites are at war and at the end, Saul has disobeyed instructions from God.

Samuel says to Saul: *Why did you not obey the LORD? Why did you become greedy, disobedient and do evil in the eyes of the LORD?"* And then the dethroning: *"Because you have rejected the word of the LORD, he has rejected you as king."* (I Samuel 15: 19, 26)

Sounds gloomy doesn't it. And you might be wondering why you're bothering reading this message.

But hold fast, there is an Upper Story message ahead. God's people are called to be different, to stand out in contrast to others by reflecting God's very character. In the transition to a kingly leader, Saul not only disobeyed God, but his actions misrepresented God. He caused the people to get the wrong idea of what God is really like.

In the Upper Story which is God's relentless pursuit to be in relationship with people, eventually there will be a different kind of king, a servant king named Jesus. He would finally bring this pursuit to the pinnacle of divine love.

But right now, you and I have daily opportunity to reflect God's character, to make sure that people get the right idea of what God is really like! From us, from how we live, speak, act, choose and trust God we have the privilege of being agents of God in transforming this world. Could there be a more holy, daily and adventuresome opportunity than that!

After the Warnings

2 Chronicles 33: 1-13

Manasseh was twelve years old when he began to reign; he reigned for fifty-five years in Jerusalem. He did what was evil in the sight of the Lord, according to the abominable practices of the nations whom the Lord drove out before the people of Israel. For he rebuilt the high places that his father Hezekiah had pulled down, and erected altars to the Baals, made sacred poles, worshipped all the host of heaven, and served them. He built altars in the house of the Lord, of which the Lord had said, 'In Jerusalem shall my name be forever.' He built altars for all the host of heaven in the two courts of the house of the Lord. He made his son pass through fire in the valley of the son of Hinnom, practiced soothsaying and augury and sorcery, and dealt with mediums and with wizards. He did much evil in the sight of the Lord, provoking him to anger. The carved image of the idol that he had made he set in the house of God, of which God said to David and to his son Solomon, 'In this house, and in Jerusalem, which I have chosen out of all the tribes of Israel, I will put my name for ever; I will never again remove the feet of Israel from the land that I appointed for your ancestors, if only they will be careful to do all that I have commanded them, all the law, the statutes, and the ordinances given through Moses.' Manasseh misled Judah and the inhabitants of Jerusalem, so that they did more evil than the nations whom the Lord had destroyed before the people of Israel.

The Lord spoke to Manasseh and to his people, but they gave no heed. Therefore, the Lord brought against them the commanders of the army of the king of Assyria, who took Manasseh captive in manacles, bound him with fetters, and brought him to Babylon. While he was in distress, he entreated the favor of the Lord his God and humbled himself greatly before the God of his ancestors. He prayed to him, and God received his entreaty, heard his plea, and restored him again to Jerusalem and to his kingdom. Then Manasseh knew that the Lord indeed was God.

Dear Friends, grace and peace be with you.

The Titanic was four days into its maiden voyage in April 1912 when Captain Edward Smith received warnings of sea ice ahead. It was still morning when the first warning came from the "Caronia," another passenger ship. Captain Smith posted the message on the bridge before leading a religious service for the passengers in first class. The second warning came in the afternoon from another ship. In the evening four more warnings urging the Titanic to change course or face disaster were ignored. At that point, it was reported the telegraphic operators were too busy handling personal messages coming in for the passengers than to pay attention to the warnings.

The ship was travelling near maximum speed when lookouts sighted the iceberg. Unable to turn quickly, the Titanic suffered a glancing blow that buckled her starboard side.

In less than three hours, the Titanic sank resulting in the deaths of more than 1,500 people, including Captain Smith. It remains among the deadliest maritime disasters in peacetime history.

Why do people ignore warnings until it's too late? I've been wondering why. Are we so occupied with our own agendas that we don't hear the warnings? Are we so undisciplined that we don't want to do the work of changing to avoid the consequences? Or are the denial systems inside us so powerful that we cannot accept reality and truth?

God could have been asking the same of the people we're reading about in the Old Testament. The story shows us that people of long ago were very powerfully able to ignore the warnings God sent through the prophets.

In the middle of the Old Testament, God's patience seems to be at an end. The northern kingdom has fallen. The southern kingdom has not so far, because King Hezekiah has been faithful to God.

When Hezekiah dies, his 12-year-old son Manasseh takes over. "Like father, like son" did not apply here. Manasseh quickly destroys all allegiance to God and rebuilds the idols that his father had destroyed. Manasseh is evil. We read in 2 Kings 2:*16* *"He sacrificed his own son in the fire."*

At this point God was angry! There would be no more warnings.

Consider this warning from God: *"I am going to bring such disaster on Jerusalem and Judah that the ears of everyone who hears of it will tingle."* (2 Kings 21:12) God's going to let the chips fall as they may.

Time is running out for the people of the Southern Kingdom. There seems to be no stopping them from achieving disaster. Manasseh won't change his ways, so God lets him be captured by the Assyrian king and led off to Babylon in utter humiliation. There's part of me that says, "Good move, God. This guy had plenty of chances to change his ways."

But while locked up, Manasseh has a change of heart. He prays to God and get this, God listens! Manasseh wants another chance to get back to Jerusalem and be a good king for the southern kingdom.

Now, if you were God, what would you do? Give Manasseh an ankle bracelet and 5 years of home-based confinement, then lifetime parole? I would have been inclined to just keep him locked up for good. But after God listens to evil Manasseh and his supposed change of heart, God responds. With mercy! God has mercy, compassion on him and eventually allows Manasseh to return to Jerusalem.

For a while, things go better in the Southern Kingdom. The people rediscover the Book of Moses that had been given to their ancestors to guide their lives and relationship with God. But eventually the people would not stay the course. They ignored the prophet's warnings. So, God let happen what God said would happen -- foreign armies capture the Southern Kingdom and the people are carried off into captivity.

Such a disappointment, isn't it? Warnings ignored again. The consequences enacted, and they seem almost fair, wouldn't you say?

The Old Testament and its recurring disappointment, destruction, and people denying doing things as God directed gets old doesn't it? We get caught up in the dismal story line and the people's destructive actions too, and we begin to lump God into this as well. God seems to be almost as disappointing and destructive.

Now, God does play a part in bringing about consequences. But if we allow our minds and our eyes to stay in the Lower Story, we easily miss the Upper Story where God is amazingly forgiving.

So, with the Southern kingdom in ruins and the people scattered, what does God do?

God tries again. This time there are two prophets, Ezekiel and Jeremiah. They're each assigned to pursue the remnants of God's people. Ezekiel shares a vision of the people coming back from exile. It's a vision of a valley of dry bones that come together with tendons and muscles and organs and skin until a multitude of people are standing there – with God breathing life back into them. Ezekiel speaks for God: *"I will gather you from all the countries and bring you back into your own land. I will sprinkle clean water on you, and you will be clean; I will cleanse you from all your impurities and from all your idols. I will give you a new heart and put a new spirit in you...You will be my people, and I will be your God."* Jeremiah 36:24-26,28). Forgiveness. Hope. For the people. From God.

Jeremiah calls the people back to God as he speaks to those captive in Babylon. He hints at a new covenant that will come from God, a Messiah, a Savior! Jeremiah says to the people who have ignored the warnings: *"The days are surely coming, says the Lord, when I will make a new covenant with the house of Israel and the house of Judah. It will not be like the covenant that I made with their ancestors when I took them by the hand to bring them out of the land of Egypt – a covenant that they broke, ... But this is the covenant that I will make...: I will put my law within them, and I will write it on their hearts; and I will be their God and they shall be my people...for I will forgive their iniquity and remember their sin no more."* (Jeremiah 31:31-34)

God uses both prophets to repeat the message of the Upper Story: *I want to live with you and will make a way for you to come back to me.* So, after ignoring the warnings and experiencing the consequences of their bad choices, Jeremiah and Ezekiel tell the people their time of exile was temporary, something amazingly better will come for them. Because of God. Because of God's mercy, Because of God's amazingly forgiving and eternally hopeful pursuits of people. That includes you and me, and every person on

this earth that longs to hear a tender, merciful word from
God, too. Amen.

All Is Calm, All Is Bright

Luke 2:1-20
*In those days a decree went out from Emperor Augustus
that all the world should be registered. This was the first
registration and was taken while Quirinius was governor of
Syria. All went to their own towns to be registered. Joseph
also went from the town of Nazareth in Galilee to Judea, to
the city of David called Bethlehem, because he was
descended from the house and family of David. He went to
be registered with Mary, to whom he was engaged and who
was expecting a child. While they were there, the time came
for her to deliver her child. And she gave birth to her
firstborn son and wrapped him in bands of cloth, and laid
him in a manger, because there was no place for them in
the inn.*

*In that region there were shepherds living in the fields,
keeping watch over their flock by night. Then an angel of
the Lord stood before them, and the glory of the Lord shone
around them, and they were terrified. But the angel said to
them, 'Do not be afraid; for see—I am bringing you good
news of great joy for all the people: to you is born this day
in the city of David a Savior, who is the Messiah, the Lord.
This will be a sign for you: you will find a child wrapped in
bands of cloth and lying in a manger.' And suddenly there
was with the angel a multitude of the heavenly host,
praising God and saying,*

Glory to God in the highest heaven,
    and on earth peace among those whom he favors!'

When the angels had left them and gone into heaven, the shepherds said to one another, 'Let us go now to Bethlehem and see this thing that has taken place, which the Lord has made known to us.' So, they went with haste and found Mary and Joseph, and the child lying in the manger. When they saw this, they made known what had been told them about this child; and all who heard it were amazed at what the shepherds told them. But Mary treasured all these words and pondered them in her heart. The shepherds returned, glorifying and praising God for all they had heard and seen, as it had been told them.

Dear Friends, may the announcement of the angel and the hope of God coming to this world be a source of peace and joy for you this night, this weekend and throughout all your days.

I have at home a stack of over 100 Christmas cards that have come to my mail box in recent weeks. Probably half of them bear the greeting, "Peace on earth." Peace is a wonderful thing to wish someone. It is a blessed thing for which to hope, primarily because it seems to be in such short supply.

Glance around our world. There are so many glaring situations void of peace. War, terrorism, earthquakes, famine, genocide. In many of situations, the division is waged under the banner of "God", or "right" or "truth". One looks at the Middle East and it is easy to see the battle between the Christian West versus the Islamic East. Perhaps we need the angels to come again this night.

Angels might usefully do less singing and a bit more to resist war, civil strife, famine and death.

We could use the peace that the angel announced that night so long ago. That Christmas wish can ring hollow in a time of war and natural disaster.

On Christmas Eve I sense a peace. Having been assaulted by commercialism and driven by culturally imposed expectation surrounding this holiday for many weeks, we have come to the quiet of this evening. This is a night we all need a little peace, isn't it?

While we sit in this lovely place and time on Christmas Eve, gathered before red poinsettias and green trees, I sense peace. Our choir and orchestra have spent weeks tuning up for this one night. The ushers have handed out candles and rounded up a few extra fire extinguishers. At the center of it all we sing and pray, and we dare to claim that "all is calm, all is bright."

We do it, of course, because that is the proclamation of the angels. "Glory to God in the highest heaven, and on earth peace to all people." At the center of the Christmas story is the announcement that God has given peace to the earth. Peace is not a vain dream or a vague hope. Peace is already here. But what kind of peace are we talking about?

- If peace means the ability to get along with others, we are anxious for it.

- If peace is considered on a global scale, we know so little of it.

- If peace is merely a matter of being nice to people with whom we disagree, maybe we could do it. Yet disagreement and discord in families and relationships can be so complex and long-standing.

- If the peace of Christmas refers to the ability to find some serenity within our own souls, we are ready for it.

There are hidden wounds from childhood, which re-emerge this time every year. Life can fracture us. Maybe that's why coming together on Christmas Eve has a particular feel to it. Perhaps we hope the old stories and favorite songs will bless us with personal peace.

Yet, the peace announced by angels was a different kind of peace. The angels did not announce peace to shepherds who fought with one another. They did not speak peace to troubled herdsmen whose hearts were heavy because of family divisions or divorce. When the angels spoke of peace, they broke the silence from God. They shattered the darkness with news of a Savior. From the highest place in the creation, they announced God has come to make peace with all creation. God has moved toward sinful, destructive people with purely peaceful intentions. Can you understand the depth of that announcement? The angels came to say:

- God has spoken to us;

- God has kind intentions toward us;

- God, who made heaven and earth has come among us to redeem and reconcile.

Listen. The angel announced good news for all people. The angel said, "God has come to you." What a remarkable thing to say to a group of anonymous shepherds. Shepherds in that time had hard lives. They wandered from place to place and depended on the land for survival. As the shepherds heard the good news, it did not remove them from troubles in the world. When the night is over, they are still nameless. And yet, a word of peace is spoken to them.

It is a remarkable thing for angels to announce peace to us, because it does not deny the troubles and dangers we face. Neither does it turn aside from the pain still evident in God's creation. God's peace comes amid our trouble and pain to assure us that "all is calm, all is bright." Have you ever experienced that peace?

An elderly woman was going through a great deal of physical pain. Physicians and physical therapists told her that she would not get well. She faced a long painful decline. One night in December, however, a choir of Lutheran angels appeared in her driveway to sing carols. She opened the door just in time to hear these words,

"How silently, how silently, the wondrous gift is given!
So, God imparts to human hearts the blessings of his heaven.

No ear can hear his coming, but in this world of sin, where meek souls will receive him,
still the dear Christ enters in.[1]"

The frail woman listened to those words, waved goodbye, and shut the door expecting aches and pains. In that moment, she felt a tranquility she had not known in months. Hobbling up the stairs, the aches and pains returned. Yet something was different.

That is the peace announced to us on Christmas. It is not the absence of pain, but serenity in the midst of stress. Peace is the momentary yet unmistakable awareness that God is present with this world. Peace is the fleeting, but very real insight that, beyond all our troubles, "all is calm, all is bright." As revealed in the skies above Bethlehem, we have a God who loves us, keeps us, and comes to fill us with the peace of the Holy Spirit. The birth of Jesus has changed the world. God has come.

The news of the angels is good, no matter what the circumstances around you or the condition of your heart. God, in Christ comes to us, not to shield us from the harshness of life, but to give us the courage and strength to bear it. God comes not to snatch us away from the conflict of life, but to give us peace-- divine peace by which we may be calmly steadfast, and in turn able to bring to this torn world, the healing that is peace.

---

[1] Lutheran Book of Worship, Augsburg Publishing, 1978, #65

As One Without Authority

Matthew 21:33-39
'Listen to another parable. There was a landowner who planted a vineyard, put a fence around it, dug a wine press in it, and built a watch-tower. Then he leased it to tenants and went to another country. When the harvest time had come, he sent his slaves to the tenants to collect his produce. But the tenants seized his slaves and beat one, killed another, and stoned another. Again, he sent other slaves, more than the first; and they treated them in the same way. Finally, he sent his son to them, saying, "They will respect my son." But when the tenants saw the son, they said to themselves, "This is the heir; come, let us kill him and get his inheritance." So, they seized him, threw him out of the vineyard, and killed him.

Dear Friends:

In the past few weeks I have had the opportunity to visit one on one with a couple dozen of high school sophomores preparing for their Affirmation of Baptism (confirmation) coming up next month. It is always a pleasure to visit with these teenagers. One of the things, perhaps the one really big thing they are all looking forward to at this point in their lives, is getting their driver's license. It brings back memories when I listen to these students tell about Driver's Education.

My driver's education instruction is something I remember well. My instructor, Bob Tone was a noted and highly-respected basketball coach in the 60's. He was also my slalom waterskiing coach and good friend of my parents. I had to behave in his class. The day he took me out to learn slalom skiing he told me right up front before I ever got wet: "Kurt, you are going to do this today and we are not coming back to shore until you do." While his goal was clear and his authority high, I knew Bob was going to be fair and firm. Bob's goal with each of his driving students was to prepare us to be confident, safe drivers, ready upon the day of passing the road test, to drive in the thick of traffic in Los Angeles or New York. Believe me, he applied his best coaching skills and discipline in teaching me to drive.

One of the most difficult things I struggled to learn was making accurate left turns. I had to do them perfectly to please Bob Tone. From the stop position at an intersection, the left side of the car had to be perfectly aligned with the center line. Taking off from that point, the car needed to make a perfect 45-degree curve so that after the left turn, the left side of the car had to be perfectly along the center line of the street. To swing too wide could send the car into the right lane and other traffic or into the parking area and a major fender collision. I know it sounds simple, but I just couldn't do it to Bob's standards. So, one day he said in his firm and concise way: "Kurt, you are going to turn left now. Close your eyes and just do what I say." So, with eyes closed, a slight shake in my hands, and a sizeable lump in my throat, I followed his commands and made the turn, not opening my eyes until given permission. And you know what, it worked. With a slight smile and a twinkle in his eye, Bob said, "See Kurt, you can do it. Just follow what I say." Bob's authority as a teacher and coach is something I always respected.

There have been many good authorities in my life. My parents, many teachers, pastors, friends – they've all been helpful and fair and have taught me well. Who have been authorities in your life?

Earlier this week I had the opportunity to listen to many authorities in major leadership roles in the Christian church. Millard Fuller, the founder and leader of Habitat for Humanity International; authors Max Lucado and Ken Blanchard of the "One Minute Manager" book and Joni Erickson-Tata, a quadriplegic who has dedicated her life to serving people with disabilities since a diving accident in 1967. They all possess a spirit of authority based squarely on Christian belief and compassion for people. Now whether you're a student, parent, a senior citizen, teacher, business-person, health professional – you benefit from authorities who lead, teach, and guide you with fairness and goodness.

This reading from Matthew is about authority-- God's authority. Like every story in the Bible, I believe we first and foremost need to ask, "What do we learn about God in this story?" This reading tells us some magnificent things about God.

Just days before Jesus was betrayed and crucified, the religious and government leaders questioned Jesus about his authority. They said "Jesus, by what authority do you go around healing people, giving them their sight, raising them from death and how is it that you call yourself God's spokesman." Jesus answered in a way he typically does, he tells a story.

Now, a little heads-up here. This story may unsettle you. Here's how Jesus answered.

There was a vineyard owned by a gracious man. For our purposes, let's make it a big garden. Picture that in your mind. The owner planted the garden, put a fence around it and rented it out to a group of tenants. Next, the owner headed up north to the cabin to enjoy the summer.

All summer, the renters enjoy the garden. Now, they do not own it mind you, and they have done nothing to improve it. But the renters enjoy the produce, until one day when the owner sends the collection agents.

The renters act as if they were in charge and had authority over the garden. They shamefully beat and kill the collection agents.

The owner up north at the cabin gets news of this awful violence. But unlike you and me, he does not call the police to have the renegade renters arrested. Instead, he sends a larger delegation of collection agents. Again, the renters beat, kick and kill the collection agents.

The owner up north at the cabin gets the news of a second massacre in his garden. But he does not call the police or hire a private investigator or a high-powered attorney to get these hoodlums out of his garden. Instead, he tries a third time to collect the rent. But this time he says to himself: "Oh my, these people need someone with more authority. I will send my son to collect the rent." Next, he summons his son saying, "Harold, my boy, you go and collect the rent for my garden."

So, the son leaves the cabin up north and goes down to the garden to collect the rent. By this time the renters are even more set on keeping the garden and it's produce for themselves. When they see the owner's son they say: "Aha, this is the son. He is in line to inherit the garden. Let's kill him too, and then we will inherit this garden and it will be ours forever." So, they killed him.

That is the end of the story. It is an awful story at face value. If you are a person who upholds right and wrong, who honors the law, then you have every right to be sickened by the rotten renters. But probably you are aghast at the owner who is downright spineless and wimpy. Here he is the guy with the authority. He owns the land. He arranged for the renters. He had every right to collect the rent and he let his employees suffer and be killed because he did not get in there and enact justice. Do you wish the owner of the garden had done something to right the wrong?

Well my friends, this is a story about our God. God is the owner of the garden. You and I are the renters. Now how do you like this story? How do you like this God? Here is a seemingly powerless God, as one without authority. God comes across being way, way too tolerant-- almost a doormat kind of God. God's authority in this story is weaker than an icicle in April.

I sometimes wish God exercised more authority in our world. Think of it, if God would just own up to God's rightful authority, there would not be people shooting our kids in high schools and churches. If God had more authority, there would not be earthquakes crushing thousands to death. If God had merely flicked Slobodan Milosevic off the globe on New Year's Day, thousands of Serbs wouldn't have been murdered this year and the USA would have saved millions of dollars in military spending. It seems like God should step up and show us some power. God should exercise some authority.

I would like God to have more authority in my personal life and yours, too. I wish God would get to some quick and specific healing for diseases and addictions. I wish God would step up to the plate to fix breaking marriages, straighten out wayward children and conflicted families. I would like a God who had more authority than I see in this story Jesus told.

Christian author, Phillip Yancey, tells of meeting with the editors of Pravda at the time the Soviet Empire was crumbling a few years ago. People in Russia were reveling in new found freedoms to act and speak. The editors of Pravda, the newspaper of the Communist Party was seeing circulation plummet and they were shaken. They asked Yancey: "Your Christian faith and our dear communism share ideals like justice, equality, harmony – yet we are going through a nightmare. Why? We don't know how to motivate people to show compassion. We tried raising money for the children of Chernobyl, but people here would rather spend money on drink. How do you Christians reform and motivate people? How do you get them to be good?

Seventy-four years of communism had proved beyond all doubt that goodness could not be laid down by law or forced with authority. Yancey said, "I left Russia with the strong sense that we Christians would do well to relearn a basic lesson about God. God's goodness cannot be imposed from the outside, it cannot be forced with power or authority, it must grow internally, from the bottom up."

The owner of the garden was magnificently restrained in the face of the evil renters. You see, God truly loved the garden and everything in it and his Son. So, God went so far as to give his son to suffer and die so that we might begin to grasp just how much we're loved. From the bottom up, out of violence, suffering and even death itself, God showed us that he truly has authority over everything in this life and this world. For from out of the despair of suffering and death, God raised his son to life and promises us life, too. Now how's that for authority! Amen.

Bowling Alone No More

Matthew 28:16-20
Now the eleven disciples went to Galilee, to the mountain to which Jesus had directed them. When they saw him, they worshipped him; but some doubted. And Jesus came and said to them, 'All authority in heaven and on earth has been given to me. Go therefore and make disciples of all nations, baptizing them in the name of the Father and of the Son and of the Holy Spirit, and teaching them to obey everything that I have commanded you. And remember, I am with you always, to the end of the age.'

Dear Sisters and Brothers in Christ, grace and peace be with you all.

Bowling Alone: The Collapse and Revival of American Community, is a book by Harvard professor, Robert Putnam. It is a fascinating account of the largest study ever conducted on the way Americans have walked away from organizations and other forms of community since the 1950's. Drawing evidence from nearly a half-a-million interviews over 25 years, Putnam's research shows that Americans are increasingly disconnected from each other.

"Bowling Alone" traces membership declines in voluntary groups like civic and service clubs (Rotary and Kiwanis and the like), PTA, professional associations, even decline in churches and synagogues. From his study,

Putnam says Americans started walking away from organization a few decades ago and today we're bowling alone like never before.

"Bowling Alone" does not just apply to organizations. Putnam's research shows that the privatization of leisure means we meet with friends less frequently, we know fewer of our neighbors, and socialize with our families less often.

Putnam concludes that the level of community in America is at its lowest point. "For the past 25 years American society has experienced a steady decline of what sociologists call 'social capital', a sense of connectedness and community. The danger in declining is that the very fabric of our connections with each other, has plummeted, impoverishing our lives and communities", including churches.

Has anyone said to you "It's all about relationships?" I had a friend say that recently, though it was not the first time I have heard it said. Relationships are helpful in all aspects of life.

While the level of connectedness between people in our society has dropped, our need for relationships and the connections they provide has not. It is healthy for us to have relationships which connect us to community life. In fact, it is the way God designed us and it's part of being an image bearer of God. Relationships and community originate right from the heart of God.

The Christian church teaches of God who is in relationship with God's self. In the concept of the Trinity, we embrace God as three expressions: Creator, Redeemer and Spirit. In understanding God together as all three, there is relationship, connectedness and community. God is God's own community. God enjoys connections and relationship.

In the biblical account of creation in Genesis, as God creates, we learn how interested God is in relationship with people. God says: "Let us make humankind in our image." (Genesis 1:26). Take a good look at that statement. Do you wonder who the "us" and the "our" is here? Right at the start, it seems that God was already relational with God's self.

Then later when God is concerned about the first human being alone God says: "It is not good for the man to be alone." (Genesis 2:18) Looking at that statement do you wonder who God is talking to? At the very beginning of creation, the Bible gives us a glimpse of God concerned about being in relationship with us.

When we turn to the stories of Jesus, we see him as a God who was always connecting with people. He loved to eat with others. He developed close friendships. Jesus showed that no one was excluded from relationship with him and he intentionally sought out people who were overlooked by others, prostitutes, beggars, handicapped people and thieves. Jesus resisted every social norm of his day that belittled or excluded or sidelined people. In Jesus, we see a relational God who knew that life is about relationships.

Well, so what? What difference does it make to you and me that God is relational? I hope it makes it a bit easier to believe in a God who cares about our lives and what we go through when we understand God's own desire for relationships. It helps me to know that God isn't some detached, powerful being uninterested in me personally, and you as well. When I think about God's heart for relationships, then I get excited about what Christian congregations have to offer. The church is an organization important to American life and can provide relationships and healthy community so that fewer people bowl alone.

Richard Lischer in his book **Open Secrets: A Spiritual Journey Through a Country Church** writes of relationships that come out of a community of people who choose to be part of a church. He includes a story of a little girl blessed greatly by relationship with a church.

Amy was a kid with a smile that never seemed to be absent from her face. When she was four years of age, Amy's parents learned she had cerebral palsy; and along with the diagnosis, they received a prescription for intense physical therapy. Every day for eight hours, seven days a week, a team of four volunteers was needed to stretch and manipulate Amy's neck and arms, hands and legs to train her muscles to work together.

This regimen of physical therapy was more than Amy's parents could afford and more than they could do themselves. Even with grandparents, aunts and uncles, they couldn't provide Amy the 56 hours a week. Because Amy's family had invested in being part of a community of faith, the people of their church pitched in. At first it was mainly other moms who showed up to treat Amy. But soon dads came to help and before long there were farmers, mechanics, retirees, and teenagers who showed up having learned about Amy in their church bulletin. Whenever they came, they did the therapy, and they loved her. Amy's father credited that for her smile.

The physical therapy itself lasted less than a year, but the congregation saw it as a miracle, not so much a miracle of a cure but the miracle of community, marked by cooperation and compassion made real. People coming to help eight hours a day seven days a week formed a community of love and concern that wouldn't have been possible without the community of the church.

It's all about relationships and community and stories like Amy's that warm our hearts. But back to "Bowling Alone." The decline in participation with voluntary groups and organizations and the increasing reality of our disconnectedness from others, affects churches, too.

Perhaps you know someone, maybe even a family member who sees little or no value in being part of a faith community. Perhaps they say, "I'm spiritual but not religious" and they have reasons they stay away from religious organizations, even though they admit to a belief in God. Yet they've chosen to go it alone, disconnected by choice from meaningful communities of faith.

This reality has serious impact on churches and people who know there is meaningful benefit from choosing to be part of a faith community.

Unfortunately, there are people who have been deeply hurt and given good reason to bowl alone spiritually because of clergy misconduct or judgmental attitudes and actions toward them. How crucial it is then for us to actively extend to all people welcoming hospitality; to open ourselves to honest, open conversation where we first listen intently to people who choose to stand apart from faith communities.

Then I think about God, our wonderfully relational God and I imagine how God's heart must hurt over all this division and decline. I wonder what does God want us to do? How you answer is truly important for the people in your life who are bowling alone.

My friends, if you know the God who loves and demonstrates relationship and community, then go and tell others. Find the people who admit to being spiritual but not religious and love them into relationship with a faith community. Show them a community that genuinely strives to represent the heart of a relational God and offers hope and forgiving love. May it be, that we, as representatives of

God, the Trinity: Creator, Redeemer, and Spirit, see to it that no one ever has reason or feels the need to bowl alone.

Contrasting Banquets

Mark 6:14-29

King Herod heard of it, for Jesus' name had become known. Some were saying, 'John the baptizer has been raised from the dead; and for this reason these powers are at work in him.' But others said, 'It is Elijah.' And others said, 'It is a prophet, like one of the prophets of old.' But when Herod heard of it, he said, 'John, whom I beheaded, has been raised.'

For Herod himself had sent men who arrested John, bound him, and put him in prison on account of Herodias, his brother Philip's wife, because Herod had married her. For John had been telling Herod, 'It is not lawful for you to have your brother's wife.' And Herodias had a grudge against him and wanted to kill him. But she could not, for Herod feared John, knowing that he was a righteous and holy man, and he protected him. When he heard him, he was greatly perplexed; and yet he liked to listen to him. But an opportunity came when Herod on his birthday gave a banquet for his courtiers and officers and for the leaders of Galilee. When his daughter Herodias came in and danced, she pleased Herod and his guests; and the king said to the girl, 'Ask me for whatever you wish, and I will give it.' And he solemnly swore to her, 'Whatever you ask me, I will give you, even half of my kingdom.' She went out and said to her mother, 'What should I ask for?' She replied, 'The head of John the baptizer.' Immediately she rushed back to the king and requested, 'I want you to give me at once the head of

John the Baptist on a platter.' The king was deeply grieved; yet out of regard for his oaths and for the guests, he did not want to refuse her. Immediately the king sent a soldier of the guard with orders to bring John's head. He went and beheaded him in the prison, brought his head on a platter, and gave it to the girl. Then the girl gave it to her mother. When his disciples heard about it, they came and took his body, and laid it in a tomb.

Dear Sisters and Brothers in Christ, grace and peace be with you all.

This is one of the more disturbing stories in the New Testament. There are two main characters. The first is John the Baptist, who was sent by God to prepare the way for Jesus. The other is Herod Antipas. He's a low-level king of the Roman Empire in charge of the territory where Jesus and his disciples have become quite popular as they conduct miracles and healings.

Herod is scared. He's scared because he's seeing more and more people flocking to Jesus and the disciples, who are busy teaching and healing in the name of God. In his fear he wonders if Jesus is John the Baptist back from the dead. But how could that be? Herod had thrown John in prison and later had him executed. This biblical story today flashes back to the sordid details of that murder.

The night of John's death Herod is throwing birthday banquet for himself. He's invited people of status, and those who needed to be reminded of his power and authority. The entertainment for the evening is provided by Herod's step-daughter, who is actually his niece. Herod, you see, had married his brother's ex-wife Herodias, after having an affair with her. This was a major offense in that culture and John the Baptist had spoken to Herod and Herodias about it. That's why John was thrown in jail.

As the girl dances, Herod swoons with delight. When she finishes, he makes a sweeping offer to her that no parent should ever make to a child: "Ask me for whatever you wish, and I'll give it to you." Obviously, Herod was new at parenting. He probably never made this mistake again.

The girl, befuddled by this stupendous offer, runs to her mother and asks for help in choosing what wish to make. Herodias, who has hated John ever since he called her out during the affair, sees a chance for her dream to come true. His judging condemnation of her behavior had so angered the blushing bride she was determined to destroy him, if given a chance. She wasn't content to simply have John in jail. It's believed that Herod put John in jail to keep his wife from killing him, a kind of protective custody. Herod is content just locking John up. He considers John to be a man of sincerity and goodness. The Bible tells us that Herod liked to listen to John telling about God.

Back to the birthday party. The girl runs back to Herod after consulting with her mother, and in front of all the party attendees says, "I want the head of John the Baptist – and put it on a platter." Where the girl got the idea of the serving piece for the head is unknown, but it did make for a most startling visual for the conclusion of the banquet.

Herod must have swallowed hard as the girl's wish echoed across the banquet hall. I'd like to think old Herod's head nearly burst as he felt the screeching collision of his values, morals and sense of right and wrong slamming inside his skull. But because of his ridiculous promise to this step-daughter, and because he had to show he was a man of his word, not weak, and because he had to save face with the guests, the request of a sassy teenager was granted. John lost his head.

Shocking, isn't it? This biblical story isn't one you want to read to your children or grandchildren while they sit on your lap. It's not one of those passages to return to again and again to be comforted. I cannot detect a single note of joy or hope anywhere in it. Can you? Rather, this is a story about the depths of human depravity and the horrors of how people with power sometimes treat other people.

This is one of a very few stories in the Gospel of Mark in which Jesus is never mentioned. But Jesus is key to understanding the story. And that my friends, is where there is some application for your life and mine. There is a point to having this horrible story as part of our wonderful worship of God this summer morning.

Although Jesus is never mentioned, this story is presented at a point where his fame and success is growing exponentially. So Mark, as he is telling us about Jesus and his growing popularity, takes us back to the events which result in John's murder. John's popularity and his determination to speak the truth to power results in his destruction. It will be no different for Jesus. To visit this disturbing story of a beheading is a foreshadowing of Jesus' death at the hands of the powerful. They are people who are fearful and threatened by Jesus' popularity and his judgement upon those who use their power to oppress.

We still live in a world where those entrusted with political power live in fear that their authority will be challenged. Leaders in our world are rarely as outwardly wicked as Herod, but they are often just as spineless, committed to expediency, and willing to compromise truth, justice, and compassion if they think it will win some votes and or secure their position of power.

I have entitled this message "Contrasting Banquet" because after this story of the birthday banquet replete with a beheading, Mark tells us of another banquet. It is the story of Jesus' feeding the 5,000. Mark is a very deliberate writer; he wants us to sense the contrast in the stories of these two different dinners. While Herod's was a banquet of death, we will realize next week that Jesus offers us a banquet of life.

Herod could have made a different choice that evening. But power, prestige, and self-aggrandizement had replaced God in his life. Though he loved to listen to John the Baptist, he would not risk his reputation and the respect of the people in order to spare John's life.

Do you see the application, even the warning here? We are always in danger of making choices that undermine our faith and align us not with God's kingdom, but rather with the principalities and powers of this world.

Our lives are filled with choices. Herod chose loyalty to his kingdom and the power it afforded him. He presided over a banquet of death. Jesus calls us to belong to Him, speaking the truth no matter the cost; working as best we can to bring justice for all, and living lives of compassion and concern for those in need. Jesus calls us to live beyond ourselves. Let us strive to do so every day of our lives, with God's help. Amen.

Dangerous Memories

Esther 1

This is the story of something that happened in the time of Xerxes, the Xerxes who ruled from India to Ethiopia - 127 provinces in all. King Xerxes ruled from his royal throne in the palace complex of Susa. In the third year of his reign he gave a banquet for all his officials and ministers. The military brass of Persia and Media were also there, along with the princes and governors of the provinces.

For six months he put on exhibit the huge wealth of his empire and its stunningly beautiful royal splendors. At the conclusion of the exhibit, the king threw a weeklong party for everyone living in Susa, the capital - important and unimportant alike. The party was in the garden courtyard of the king's summer house.

The courtyard was elaborately decorated with white and blue cotton curtains tied with linen and purple cords to silver rings on marble columns. Silver and gold couches were arranged on a mosaic pavement of porphyry, marble, mother-of-pearl, and colored stones. Drinks were served in gold chalices, each chalice one-of-a-kind. The royal wine flowed freely - a generous king! The guests could drink as much as they liked - king's orders! - with waiters at their elbows to refill the drinks.

Meanwhile, Queen Vashti was throwing a separate party for women inside King Xerxes' royal palace. On the seventh day of the party, the king, high on the wine, ordered the seven eunuchs who were his personal servants to bring him Queen Vashti resplendent in her royal crown. He wanted to show off her beauty to the guests and officials. She was extremely good-looking. But Queen Vashti refused to come, refused the summons delivered by the eunuchs. The king lost his temper. Seething with anger over her insolence, the king called in his counselors, all experts in legal matters. It was the king's practice to consult his expert advisors.

Those closest to him were Carshena, Shethar, Admatha, Tarshish, Meres, Marsena, and Memucan, the seven highest-ranking princes of Persia and Media, the inner circle with access to the king's ear. He asked them what legal recourse they had against Queen Vashti for not obeying King Xerxes' summons delivered by the eunuchs.

Memucan spoke up in the council of the king and princes: "It's not only the king Queen Vashti has insulted, it's all of us, leaders and people alike in every last one of King Xerxes' provinces. The word's going to get out: 'Did you hear the latest about Queen Vashti? King Xerxes ordered her to be brought before him and she wouldn't do it!' When the women hear it, they'll start treating their husbands with contempt. The day the wives of the Persian and Mede officials get wind of the queen's insolence, they'll be out of control. Is that what we want, a country of angry women who don't know their place?

"So, if the king agrees, let him pronounce a royal ruling and have it recorded in the laws of the Persians and Medes

so that it cannot be revoked, that Vashti is permanently banned from King Xerxes' presence. And then let the king give her royal position to a woman who knows her place.

When the king's ruling becomes public knowledge throughout the kingdom, extensive as it is, every woman, regardless of her social position, will show proper respect to her husband." The king and the princes liked this.

The king did what Memucan proposed. He sent bulletins to every part of the kingdom, to each province in its own script, to each people in their own language: "Every man is master of his own house; whatever he says, goes."

Dear Sisters and Brothers in Christ, grace and peace be with you all.

This story from the Old Testament brings to us a woman we've probably never heard of. Queen Vashti is her name. The reason you probably never heard of her is because her story is a dangerous memory. Dangerous memories are things that really happened, but are too damaging, racy, painful or embarrassing to remember.

I would guess we all have stories in our families which could be classified as dangerous memories, which means that we would rather not hear or think about them, let alone pass them along to the kids. Sometimes, there are good reasons for keeping things quiet. Maybe it is better the kids don't know why Mom and Dad divorced or how Aunt

Bessie kept her family together or how grandpa made his money. But, sometimes, dangerous memories stop being dangerous when we get them out in the open and learn from them. Sometimes they can make us stronger.

The biblical story of Queen Vashti can be classified as a dangerous memory and so, perhaps that's why you have never heard of her. Yet, I think that such memories exposed can make us better people of faith striving to live out from the Upper Story of God.

Vashti makes only one appearance in the Bible. She's part of probably the biggest party ever given in the ancient world. It's a big drunken brawl hosted by the king. It was 187 days of continual Animal House-like debauchery.

King Xerxes, who ruled lands from Ethiopia to India, hosted this party for officials who worked for him in 127 provinces. The purpose of this party was not to thank his employees. It was to impress them with the splendor and pomp of his royal palace. During the six-month party the only agenda for these guys was to gorge and drink and be impressed by the king's opulence.

On day 187 of this royal bash, the king had one last bit of opulence to display: his hordes of wives. Bear in mind that in this period of history men and women lived separately. No one was allowed to look at the king's wives except the king and his eunuchs, who were, as you can figure, no threat at all. King Xerxes likes to flaunt. So, he orders his servants to bring him the ravishing Queen Vashti so that everyone can "see her beauty" which means, basically, that he wants Vashti to come out wearing only her crown; nothing else. The king wants all these men who have spent six months eating his food and drinking his wine to take a good look at his wife and to remember that this is one thing they cannot have.

Here comes the dangerous part of the story. Even though the atmosphere is as charged with testosterone as you will ever find, Queen Vashti does not do as any obedient subject of the king ought to do, when given a direct order. She does not shuck her clothes, swallow her pride, and do as she was commanded in order to keep her man happy. Queen Vashti is probably the first woman on record to say no. "No, I will not come out and make a display of myself for your benefit. No, I will not degrade myself so that you can save face in front of your friends. No, I will not do whatever you tell me to do. And most emphatically I will not do it when you have been drunk for 187 days."

The king is humiliated in front of all the men of the kingdom. He is enraged too. Word of Queen Vashti's refusing a man's command lets loose a tidal wave of rebellion among the women of the empire. Noble ladies everywhere are discovering great potential in saying no. The order of the entire kingdom is disrupted. What to do?

The king and his officials put their heads together. They ask: According to the law, what is to be done to Queen Vashti because she has not performed the command of the

King? They decide: "Let her rot. Away with Vashti and away with any woman who fails to do as her husband commands. Let another queen be chosen to take Vashti's place."

Vashti disappears; there is a recruiting call for young virgins to come and compete for the queen's title and eventually a young Jewish woman named Esther is crowned queen, as the memory of Vashti is left to rot.

However, the story of Vashti cannot be erased. Vashti may be nothing but a prologue to this Old Testament story, but she lives on in the minds of her people and Queen Esther, too. Esther will advance what Vashti had started. She speaks up and takes great risks with the king and other men to save her people, the Jews, from being annihilated. It was a bold thing for a woman to do in those days. In doing so she becomes for God's Upper Story, the right person, in the right place, at the right time.

I wonder whether Esther would have ever found the courage to do as she did, if not for the example of Vashti, the woman who first said no. In an age when women did not have a purpose other than that of being decorative and fertile, Vashti cut new ground. "No," she said, "I am more than a decorative display. I am a human being, with integrity and self-respect."

When Esther becomes Queen, she finishes what Vashti started. Together, their story is a sacred memory of how women, or any oppressed people, can overturn a world by standing against injustice, and how one resistance can give rise to another. Vashti and Esther, as biblical characters, represent more than a feminist message. This is not a story for women looking for a reason to rebel. This is a story for every person who has ever felt their integrity called into question, who has ever had to weigh the risks between their job and their self-respect, who has ever had to stand up in the face of an unjust situation and say, "No, I cannot go along with this."

I wonder what would happen if we put the story of Vashti back into circulation. Would our children have a role model for just saying no to adults who try to molest or harm them? Would our daughters muster a little more courage for just saying no to boys who pressure them to have sex when they don't want to? Would it give you and me a place to begin talking about the awkward, troubling time when we feel like we are being asked to do something that puts our integrity at risk?

It is a funny thing: We don't have many role models for saying no, especially from the Bible. It's true that Jesus put his foot down on several occasions, but we tend to think of our Christian faith in terms of saying YES--to God, to Jesus, to love, to the commands. Maybe what we need to hear is that an equally important part of our life as Christians is finding the encouragement to say NO when we need to, not because it's the easy thing to do, but because it's the right thing to do.

I like the fact that this is not a clean story. Vashti does not save the day with her great NO. In fact, she loses: They take away her crown, her position, her prestige, her good name. In the eyes of the world, when Vashti says no, she gets herself exiled. But in the eyes of God, it is something different. Vashti's courage inspires the next woman, and the next, and the next. Vashti's great NO becomes Esther's great NO, so that the Jews in the empire are not systematically murdered.

Vashti's example encourages women and men to speak up for themselves and stand with integrity. Doing so can come with a harsh cost. But from Vashti and Esther's actions and the biblical writers who remembered to pass on this dangerous memory, we benefit. Standing against oppression and speaking up for integrity has the power to change the world for the better. Who knows, but that you and I have come to this time in order to bring to this world an important "no" and some hopeful integrity, too. Amen.

Get Out of the Boat

Matthew 14:2233
Immediately Jesus made the disciples get into the boat and go on ahead to the other side, while he dismissed the crowds. And after he had dismissed the crowds, he went up the mountain by himself to pray. When evening came, he was there alone, but by this time the boat, battered by the waves, was far from the land, for the wind was against them. And early in the morning he came walking towards them on the lake. But when the disciples saw him walking on the lake, they were terrified, saying, 'It is a ghost!' And they cried out in fear. But immediately Jesus spoke to them and said, 'Take heart, it is I; do not be afraid.'

Peter answered him, 'Lord, if it is you, command me to come to you on the water.' He said, 'Come.' So, Peter got out of the boat, started walking on the water, and came towards Jesus. But when he noticed the strong wind, he became frightened, and beginning to sink, he cried out, 'Lord, save me!' Jesus immediately reached out his hand and caught him, saying to him, 'You of little faith, why did you doubt?' When they got into the boat, the wind ceased. And those in the boat worshipped him, saying, 'Truly you are the Son of God.'

Dear Friends:

Many years ago, when I was a preteen, summers were annual opportunities for adventure and exploration. Growing up on the edge of a small city, my playmates and I captured nature in ways which provided us not only great fun, but amazing opportunities to learn. Beyond the neighborhood, my family was fortunate to have property on a nearby lake at which we spent many weekends throughout the summer. There, nature was vast and the lake itself offered many opportunities to learn.

One of the most memorable learning opportunities on water occurred when I was 11. With permission to drive my dad's 14' aluminum fishing boat powered by a 9 ½ horsepower Johnson motor, I loved starting each weekend by donning the orange life-vest and exploring the lake with its bays and sand bars. One evening, my exploration was going at a notable speed and the bay I entered was one of the more populated ones. As I turned to exit the bay, either I mis-read a wave or I was distracted by someone on the shoreline or the motor coughed and surprised me, but whatever the cause, the result was I was thrown out of the boat. The boat continued around the lake. Without me. Driver-less. At full speed.

I learned many things on the water that day: a driver-less fishing boat with small motor does not go in a straight line and a circling, out of control boat draws quite a crowd of spectators.

This personal experience of fear on the water draws me to the biblical story today. I feel a keen identification with Peter and what he learned from Jesus as he got out of the boat. Peter presents us one of the greatest pictures of extreme faith in the entire Bible. Peter, the water walker.

Now, that is not what I was aspiring to that day when was 11 years old. But since then, my aspirations have changed. I hope yours will in this time together this morning.

Let's look at the story a little closer. Peter and his friends get into a boat one afternoon to cross the Sea of Galilee, just as Jesus had requested. Jesus wanted to be alone, so they were boating without him.

Sometime during the night, a violent storm came up. Peter and company fight to keep the boat upright and they're scared. This is a big storm! Then about 3am one of them spotted a shadow moving toward them on the water. The closer it got, it became apparent that it was a person walking on the water.

Well, it was not a ghost, but Jesus and he's decided it was time for the people in the boat to get to know Him better. He shouts out: "Hey guys, you can trust me. You know my character and competence. You can safely place your destiny in my hand. Take courage. It's me."

The crew in the boat did not fully grasp it yet, but amidst their fears and emotions God was visiting them in the water-walking flesh.

The Bible story doesn't tell us how 11 of the people in the boat responded to Jesus' voice. But we learn how Peter did and he's about to become a water-walker. He recognized God was present and he decided to take a big step of faith and trust God completely!

Peter blurts out: "If it is you, command me to come to you on the water." Peter asks for permission. He seeks to figure out what God wants of him. He asks, "If it is you, command me to follow your lead."

Before I go further, I want you to put yourself in the story. Picture in your mind how violent the storm was that it kept seasoned boaters struggling just to stay upright. Imagine the height of the waves and the darkness of night and no Dramamine. These were the conditions under which Peter was going to get out of the boat.

Put yourself in Peter's place. You suddenly see Jesus on the water and he's open to having you go on the adventure of your life. But at the same time, you're scared to death. What would you choose? The water or the boat?

The boat is safe and secure.

I believe there is something, someone inside you and me who tells us there is more to life than sitting in the boat. We were made for something more than avoiding risk and failure. There is something inside us that wants to walk on the water – to leave the comfort of routine existence and abandon yourself to the high adventure of following God.

So, let me ask two very important questions: What holds you back? What is your boat?

Your boat is whatever represents safety and security to you apart from God. Your boat is whatever you put your trust in, especially when life gets a little stormy. Your boat is whatever keeps you so comfortable that you don't want to give it up even if it is keeping you from joining Jesus on the water. Your boat is whatever pulls you away from the high adventure of boldly following Jesus.

You want to know what your boat is? Your fear will tell you. Just ask yourself this: What is it that most produces fear in me, especially when I think of leaving it behind and stepping out in faith?

For Kathy, her boat is a relationship. She's been involved for years with a guy whose commitment to her is ambivalent. He's sending her signals that everyone else reads clearly, that he is never going to make a commitment to her. But she is too afraid to discover his true feelings. She does not believe she could handle losing him. Her boat is shaky. But she is too scared to leave.

For Dave, his boat is his career. He has been a builder for 30 years and in his late fifties now. But he has been gnawed for decades by a sense that God was calling him into church ministry. He has quieted his conscience by giving a lot of money and doing many good things, but he cannot shake off the haunting fear that he has missed his calling. And he is afraid that perhaps it is too late.

For Doug, his boat is secrecy. He is addicted to alcohol. It is a mild addiction, or so he tells himself. He has not lost a job or a marriage so far. But he thinks no one knows. He is afraid to admit it. He is afraid to get help. Secrecy is killing him. But it is his boat.

Maybe your boat is success. That was the case of a young man in another Bible story. Jesus asked him to get out of the boat and follow, after he sold all that he had and gave the money to the poor. But the rich young man decided not to. He had a very nice boat, a yacht. It was comfortable and secure, and he liked it too much to give it up.

What is your boat? In what area of your life are you shrinking back from fully and courageously trusting God? Fear will tell you what your boat is. Leaving it may be the hardest thing you ever do.

But if you want to walk on water you have to get out of the boat.

Peter as he gets out of the boat, takes a huge step of faith. He lets go, abandoning himself utterly to the power of Jesus. And for the first time in history, an ordinary person walks on water.

Peter beams with delight. He has locked his eyes on Jesus as he moves toward Him.

Then it happens. Peter "sees the wind." The enormity of his step of faith faces reality and he starts to sink. What has really taken place is that Peter's focus has shifted from the Savior to the storm.

Do you know what it is like to see the wind? You begin a new adventure full of hope as you take a big step of faith. Maybe it is a new job; a marriage or maybe your trying to serve God in a new way. At the beginning you are full of faith. You are seeing the growth. It is exciting.

Then reality sets in. Setbacks. Oppositions. Obstacles. You see the wind and fears build. But here's a truth about water-walking. The fear will never go away. Why? Because fear and growth go together like macaroni and cheese. It's a package deal. The decision to grow always involves a choice between risk and comfort. To follow Jesus you must release comfort and security as primary values in your life. And that is sobering news to most of us, because we are into comfort!

When Peter lets fear replace faith on the water, he started to sink. But did he fail?

Someone once asked Winston Churchill what prepared him to risk political suicide by speaking out against Hitler during the mid-1930's, a time known as the years of appeasement. Churchill replied, "It was the time I had to repeat a grade in elementary school that prepared me."

"You mean you failed a year in grade school?" he was asked.

"I never failed anything in my life," Churchill replied. "I was given a second opportunity to get it right."

When Peter started to sink, Jesus was immediately there, reaching out his hand, rescuing him. And perhaps that's key learning for us as we choose to get out of the boat to more boldly follow Jesus. He's there - aware of our fears - and ready to help as we face the risks of more boldly living the life God wants for us.

My friends, God's way for growing a deep, adventuresome faith in us is by asking us to get out of the boat. If you do get out, two things will happen. First, when you start to fail and we all do, Jesus will be there to pick you up. You will not be alone. the second thing is, every so often, you will walk on the water. Amen.

Getting in on the Conversation

1 Samuel 3:1-10
The boy Samuel was serving God under Eli's direction. This was at a time when the revelation of God was rarely heard or seen.

One night Eli was sound asleep (his eyesight was very bad--he could hardly see). It was well before dawn; the sanctuary lamp was still burning. Samuel was still in bed in the Temple of God, where the Chest of God rested.

Then God called out, "Samuel, Samuel!" Then he ran to Eli saying, "I heard you call. Here I am." Eli said, "I didn't call you. Go back to bed." And so he did.

God called again, "Samuel, Samuel!" Samuel got up and went to Eli, "I heard you call. Here I am." (This all happened before Samuel knew God for himself. It was before the revelation of God had been given to him personally.)

God called again, "Samuel!"-- the third time! Yet again Samuel got up and went to Eli, "Yes? I heard you call me. Here I am." So Eli directed Samuel, "Go back and lie down. If the voice calls again, say, 'Speak, God. I'm your servant, ready to listen.'" Samuel returned to his bed.

Then God came and stood before him exactly as before, calling out, "Samuel! Samuel!" Samuel answered, "Speak. I am your servant, ready to listen."

Dear Sisters and Brothers, may the grace and peace of Christ be yours in abundance.

Just two weeks into the new year, and we are being ushered into an election season. With primary and general elections in 2012 and perhaps a recall election, too; there is one certainty we all will endure no matter our political persuasion: there will be a wide-array of voices seeking our attention.

This Bible reading from I Samuel engages us in a conversation. When you think about it, we are almost constantly in conversation, aren't we? Whether we like it or not, many voices call out to us.

The voices of people around us call us into conversation. From our children, spouse, friends and coworkers, they all have voices which make a claim on us: "Mom, can I have a cookie?" "Dear, do you have time this weekend to clean the garage?" "Dad, I had a little accident while driving home from school." "Are you free to meet me for dinner tomorrow night?" "I need this report by Friday." It is important for us to listen to the voices of people with whom we share relationships and to whom we have some accountability.

There are other "voices" which draw us into <u>ethical</u> conversations. Just looking at voices on the front page of a newspaper these days draws me into conversation:

- Officials in Haiti say the number of people now without homes has dropped to about 550,000 since an earthquake two years ago this month.

- North Korea open to suspending uranium development for nuclear purposes in exchange for US food aid.

- Forty percent of U.S. children are born to unmarried women (Pew study - Dec 19 foxnews.com)

- American CEOs pay increases between 27 and 40 % last year *(Governance Metrics International survey cited by Guardian)*.

These voices call us into conversations which engage our values, our hopes for change, and our concerns for a complicated and confusing society.

Beyond the voices of the people around us and the news of the world, we hear the voice of our own mind and soul. The voices of our fears and past sins, our loneliness or unfulfilled dreams, is heard within, in addition to the voices of deep joy, contentment, and gratitude.

So, do you agree with me that we are constantly in conversation with the people around us, the events in the world and that which is going on inside ourselves?

There is one more for the list. As people of faith, as those who claim a relationship with God, I hope we can add God's voice engaging us in conversation.

Today's Old Testament Bible reading draws us into a conversation that God initiates with a boy named Samuel.

Now, some context for this reading. Samuel is about 12 years old. His mother is Hanna and this boy is the fulfillment of her dream, because for many years she was unable to have children. In a conversation with God, Hanna promised God that if she were to be given the privilege of bearing a child, she would return the child to God's service. Samuel was born, and true to her word as soon as he was able to make it on his own, Hanna left the boy to live with and be trained by the high priest, a man named Eli.

Some background to the story. Eli is an old man. His eyesight is dimming. He has two adult sons who have gone rogue. They have earned God's dismay by cursing God and bringing shame upon Eli in his work as high priest. In turn, God is not happy with Eli because he has not done anything to reign in his two bad boys. They have also interrupted the work God has expected of Eli. It is a discouraging time. The Bible reading tells us *"The word of the Lord was rare in those days."* (I Samuel 3:1 NRSV).

Eli has been warned by God that judgment would come upon him. Yet, Eli is just too old and tired to respond in any fruitful way. However, he has his hopes pinned on Samuel to bring honor to God and benefit others.

Samuel is asleep in the temple; only Eli is around. A voice comes during night: "Samuel. Samuel."

The boy assumes it is old Eli calling. It has happened before that Eli has called out during the night. His eyesight is bad, or he probably needs help getting to the bathroom. When Samuel hears his name called he goes to the old man and says, "Eli, you called?" The old priest rolls over in his bed and says, "No, I didn't. Go back to sleep."

Samuel goes back to bed. The voice calls again: "Samuel!" Again, he returns to Eli and says "You called? What do you want?"

By now Eli is wide awake because he hasn't returned to sleep since the first time Samuel woke him. Eli has had some time to think about the voice the boy heard. He wondered if Samuel was having a dream. Or was it something more? Eli, being a faithful man and one who had been in conversation with God in his lifetime wondered if Samuel was hearing the voice of God. But Eli was not so sure. God's direct contact with human beings seemed to be a thing of the past. He had no doubt that God was involved with the lives of the people, Samuel's very birth to a woman who had been unable to bear children was the answer to a most specific prayer. But now with this second call, Eli wonders. Maybe ... just maybe. So, he says to Samuel: "No, I did not call. Go back to bed."

The puzzled twelve-year-old returns to bed. Before he can get comfortable again, the voice returns: "Samuel."

"What in the world? This is getting ridiculous," Samuel thought as he was getting up again and going back to the priest. "You called?" He wondered if Eli was playing a game with him, but it was a strange time of the night for games.

By now, Eli knows to whom the voice belongs. He turns his old gray head and those age-dimmed eyes to the boy and says, "No, I did not call. Go back and lie down. But if the voice comes again, say, 'Speak, Lord, for your servant is listening.' "

Samuel's mind is racing a mile a minute as he got back into bed. "What could God want with me?" he wondered. Samuel had never heard the voice of God. Sure enough, a fourth time it comes: "Samuel. Samuel!"

This time Samuel takes Eli's wise guidance and responds: "Speak, Lord, for your servant is listening." And the rest, as they say, is history. When the voice came again, Samuel began a conversation with God which challenged and changed the lives of Eli's people and radically changed his own life forever.

With the many voices that call to us, from those inside us and those beyond us, can you identify the voice of God? It is there. Samuel, in the silence of night was guided by a wise, spiritually mature person to hear the voice of God and get in on a conversation.

There is lots of good news in this Bible reading. There is the truth that God does speak to people and with just a little guidance, we can hear. There is the good news that no matter all the voices and constant conversation going on around us and within us, God does speak. There is the good news we see in Samuel's experience that God is persistent in getting us to listen. God is much more willing to speak than we are to listen.

I hope at this point in my message you have started a conversation with yourself asking "How can I better listen for God?" I think it is good for each of us to seek an answer that fits our place and situation in life. Here are some tips that have been fruitful for me in picking out God's voice:

1. Expect to hear God's voice. Maybe your expectations of God have been too low.

2. Stop the noise in your life. It is nearly impossible to hear God's voice amid the conversations going on around and in us. Silence is the first language of God.

3. Read how God has spoken to others. Just like this Bible story, God's Word can help us better listen for God's voice. Dedicate some quiet time each day to reading how God has spoken to others.

4. Finally, find an Eli. Find a friend who has a deep and wise awareness of God's voice and then stay close to that friend.

I hope that you will hear the voice of God amidst all the voices in your life; and then, like Samuel respond: "Speak Lord, for your servant is listening." Amen.

God's House Rules

John 2:1-12

On the third day there was a wedding in Cana of Galilee, and the mother of Jesus was there. Jesus and his disciples had also been invited to the wedding. When the wine gave out, the mother of Jesus said to him, "They have no wine." And Jesus said to her, "Woman, what concern is that to you and to me? My hour has not yet come." His mother said to the servants, "Do whatever he tells you." Now standing there were six stone water jars for the Jewish rites of purification, each holding twenty or thirty gallons. Jesus said to them, "Fill the jars with water." And they filled them up to the brim. He said to them, "Now draw some out, and take it to the chief steward." So, they took it. When the steward tasted the water that had become wine and did not know where it came from (though the servants who had drawn the water knew), the steward called the bridegroom and said to him, "Everyone serves the good wine first, and then the inferior wine after the guests have become drunk. But you have kept the good wine until now." Jesus did this, the first of his signs, in Cana of Galilee, and revealed his glory; and his disciples believed in him.

After this he went down to Capernaum with his mother, his brothers, and his disciples; and they remained there a few days.

Dear Sisters and Brothers in Christ, may the abundant grace and mercy of God be yours today and always.

During the wedding rehearsal, the groom approached the pastor with an unusual offer. "I'll give you $100 if you'll change the wedding vows. When you get to me and the part where I'm to promise to 'love, honor and obey' and 'forsaking all others, be faithful to her forever,' I'd appreciate it if you'd just leave that part out." He handed the pastor a $100 bill and walked away.

The next day during the wedding, everything was going smoothly. Then it came time came for the exchange of vows. The pastor started with the groom asking him: "Will you promise to submit yourself to her, obey her every command, and swear eternally before God and these witness that you will not ever even look at another woman, as long as you both shall live?"

The groom gulped, looked around, and said in a tiny voice, "Yes." He then leaned toward the pastor and hissed, "I thought we had a deal."

The pastor put the $100 bill into the groom's hand and whispered back, "She made me a much better offer."

Weddings, sometimes they are marked with drama and anxiety.

As we join the Bible reading today, Jesus and his mother, Mary, are at a wedding reception. There is some drama and anxiety going on when Mary exclaims to Jesus: "They have no wine. Do something Jesus."

In Mary's anxiety, I hear concerns about scarcity. "The wine is running out." You and I know the questions of scarcity that go through our minds. We wonder "Do I have enough money? Am I good enough? Do I measure up with others? Will I have enough to retire someday?

To questions of scarcity like Mary's about wine, Jesus answers with God's abundance.

Stephen Covey, author, educator, and businessman, who just died six months ago wrote this: *"People with a scarcity mentality tend to see everything in terms of winlose. Whereas people who develop an abundance mentality...are genuinely happy for the good fortune of others."*

Abundance. The word makes us think economically -- focusing on quantity, things that can be measured by dollars and numbers and bottles of wine. We think economically when we look at our paychecks and bank balances.

Yet, when it comes to Christian living, abundance is defined differently and not measured just in mere numbers. Abundance, regarding Christian faith compels us to consider life abundant from God that is to be for all people in the world.

Sallie McFague is an author and theologian. She urges people to look at what abundance means for Christian living. In her book Life Abundant: Rethinking Theology and Economy for a Planet in Peril, McFague makes the case for Christians who seriously want to live the good life as God defines it. The Christian good life, she says, is marked by sustainability, self-limitation and inclusion of all, especially the weak and vulnerable.

To help us think about living the good life--we need to put the cross in front of our minds. Think of the two parts of a cross. The vertical points us to God and reminds us of God coming to us. It's God and me we see in the vertical. The horizontal reminds us of Jesus' arms reaching out to embrace all people, all creation. It also makes us look out over to each other, all humanity and all the creation across the world. Putting the vertical and horizontal together defines the crossshaped life. Cross-shaped living means we enact our faith and actions so that they come to extend God's abundance to all people.

McFague writes that for Christians the cross-shaped life brings an alternative notion of the abundant life. For us American Christians this crossshaped life will not be primarily a vertical thought, what Christ does for us. Instead it will be a horizontal thought of what we can do for others. She writes: "We do not need so much to accept God forgiving our sins as we need to repent of the sin of our silent complicity in the impoverishment of others and the degradation of the planet." (p. 14)

This is radical stuff. Living this crossshaped life is not about a comfortable relationship with a sweet, easy God. It's not about seeing our successes as blessings from a God who likes us better. The crossshaped life involves the critical connection between the personal and the civic. The cross-shaped life means that we live out the love of God in every choice we make, the money we spend and decisions about houses and cars, entertainment and recreation, food, water, heat and light.

These choices are about numbers. Dollars. They are economic. They are also spiritual. It is God's intention that all people know life abundant. We see this truth in the life of Jesus--the one who turned water into wine, the one who sat down to table with all the wrong people and continually pointed out and lifted the poor as the first object of God's concern. It is God's intention that all life should flourish. Our task, if we choose cross-shaped living, is to tend to stewarding life abundant and bringing it to flourish in the place where God came to dwell, that is, our earth, our world.

To help us live crossshaped lives McFague offers three tools:

First: Crossshaped living starts with asking ourselves how much is enough? It follows then with practicing "enoughness." We limit our consumption of the world's resources in recognition of the needs of others who don't have those resources.

Second: Honoring God's House rules. We live in the place where God came to dwell in Jesus so think of this world as God's house where we abide by God's house rules. The rules are economic and understandable. Take only your share, clean up after yourselves and keep the house in good repair for future occupants.

Third: Find your "wild space." Wild space is that part in each one of us that does not fit the definition of the good life. In culture's definition of the good life are things like: financial success, professional status, material comforts, good health, intact family, marriage and children. Your "wild space" is where you don't fit that model of the good life

Perhaps you are not married, or you have been divorced; maybe you have no children, or you live with physical issues. Those things are not in the definition of the good life. Perhaps you or someone in your family lives with depression or addiction. Perhaps you have anxiety over financial insecurity, family divisions or estrangements, fears about not making it. These things do not fall in culture's definition of the good life, so where you do not fit is your wild space. Wild space causes us to question the definition of the good life that we can waste so much time trying to achieve, at the expense of cross-shaped living. Anything that causes us to question the definition of success and the good life is our wild space.

Knowing your wild space gives the ability to stand apart from culture's definition of the good life. Knowing your wild space helps you move to cross-shaped living and extending the radical, extravagant love of God and God's desire for all people to know life abundant.

Jesus knew his wild space. It was his wild space that allowed him to say that everybody, really everybody, is welcome at the banquet table of the kingdom of heaven. It was that wild space that allowed him to talk with prostitutes and dine with the outcasts. It was that countercultural wild space in Jesus that cost him his life and that gives us ours.

I hope you will consider your wild space, where you do not fit or choose not to buy into culture's definition of the good life. Your wild space can help you begin to recognize that which can fill your spirit and satisfy your soul. It is our wild space that allows us to question consuming more, practice "enoughness" and instead finding alternative ways to use the earth's resources and tend to God's house. Our wild space will open us to find better ways to address the massive needs of people who have no chance now for life abundant.

So, my friends, this week try living out God's love for all by every choice we make. Try out God's house rules and finally, look for your wild space. Then our questions about scarcity, about having enough can shift to: "How shall I live this new life of God's abundance, where there is enough for all?" Amen.

God's Will: Tragedy or Triumph

Luke 13: 1-9

At that very time there were some present who told him about the Galileans whose blood Pilate had mingled with their sacrifices. He asked them, 'Do you think that because these Galileans suffered in this way, they were worse sinners than all other Galileans? No, I tell you; but unless you repent, you will all perish as they did. Or those eighteen who were killed when the tower of Siloam fell on them—do you think that they were worse offenders than all the others living in Jerusalem? No, I tell you; but unless you repent, you will all perish just as they did.'

Then he told this parable: 'A man had a fig tree planted in his vineyard; and he came looking for fruit on it and found none. So, he said to the gardener, "See here! For three years I have come looking for fruit on this fig tree, and still I find none. Cut it down! Why should it be wasting the soil?" He replied, "Sir, let it alone for one more year, until I dig round it and put manure on it. If it bears fruit next year, well and good; but if not, you can cut it down." '

Dear Sisters and Brothers in Christ, may the grace and peace of God be yours in abundance.

It is hard to let God be God. We long to explain things only God can know.

A fellow pastor tells of an encounter with a mother whose child was in crisis. She was attempting to explain things beyond her ability.

While serving as a hospital chaplain the pastor received a call to sit with a mother while her five-year-old daughter was in surgery. Earlier in the week, the girl had been playing with a friend when her head began to hurt. By the time she found her mother, she could no longer see. At the hospital, a CT scan showed a large tumor was pressing on the girl's optic nerve. Surgery was scheduled for the next day.

During the surgery, the chaplain found the girl's mother sitting alone in the waiting room beside an ashtray full of cigarette butts (back in the time when smoking inside hospitals was permitted). She smelled as if she had puffed every one of them. She was staring at a patch of carpet in front of her, with eyebrows raised in a half-hypnotized look. Some minutes passed before she looked up and after some small talk, she expressed just how awful this was for her. She even explained why her daughter had this tumor.

"It's my punishment," she said. "It's my punishment for smoking these horrid cigarettes. God couldn't get my attention any other way, so God made my baby sick." Then she started crying so hard that what she said next came out like a siren: "Now I'm supposed to stop, but I can't stop. I'm going to kill my own child!"

Even seasoned pastors find such words hard to hear. At this point, a brave pastor finds some way to offer a remedial understanding of God. So, the chaplain replied: "I don't believe in a God like that. The God I know wouldn't do something like that."

However, this response messed with the mother's thinking that her daughter's tumor was due to God's anger over her smoking. However miserable it made her to think her smoking led to God putting a tumor in her daughter's brain, she preferred a punishing God to an absent or capricious one. While the pastor could understand a loving God, despite tragedy and crisis like a young girl with a brain tumor, at that moment the mother could not. In her thinking, there had to be a God-given reason her daughter had a tumor. She was even willing to be the reason. At least that way she could get a grip on the catastrophe.

Have you thought in this way? Have you heard people attribute health crises, tragedies, even death to God? It's not uncommon when a crisis arises, that we go looking for causes. We scrutinize our actions or our inactions--we go hunting for some cause to explain the effect in hopes that we can stop causing it. What we crave in these experiences, above all, is control over the chaos of this world and the suffering in life.

From generation to generation, people have sought to make sense of things that make no sense. We look for causes for suffering and tragedy or we blame God. We say things about God or put words into God's mouth that are our own, rather than God's.

Some years ago, William Sloan Coffin was the pastor of Riverside Church in New York City. After his son Alex died in a car accident, Coffin shared a sermon on cause and effect thinking. Alex drowned after he lost control of his car during a terrible storm and it careened into Boston Harbor. The following Sunday, Rev. Coffin spoke about his son's death. He thanked all the people for their expressions of sympathy, for food brought to their home. But he also raged; he raged about well-meaning folks who had hinted that Alex's death was God's will. "I knew the anger would do me good," he said.

Then he went on: "Do you think it was God's will that Alex never fixed that lousy windshield wiper...that he was probably driving too fast in such a storm, that he probably had a couple of beers too many? Do you think it was God's will that there were no street lights along that stretch of the road and no guard rail along Boston Harbor? The one thing that should never be said when someone dies is, 'It is the will of God' or that 'God wanted him or her more.'"

Coffin continued: "Never do we know enough to say that. My own consolation lies in knowing that when the waves closed over the sinking car, God's heart was the first of all our hearts to break."

It's hard to let God be God. We long to make sense of senseless tragedies and search for reasons even when there are none. Or when bad things happen, we pin blame on God. Sometime people think terrible events are prompted by extraordinary sinfulness. People constantly ask why God sends (or at least permits) terrible things to happen. People often blame God for tragedy.

Jesus anticipated these kinds of questions and this kind of thinking in today's Bible reading. Two terrible tragedies had happened in Jerusalem: the first one was in the temple; the second tragedy was near the pool of Siloam, just outside the city wall of Jerusalem. In the first instance, Pilate, the Roman governor, had killed some Galileans (these were people who protested the Roman Empire's taxes). They were killed while making sacrifices in the temple. In the second incident, a tower fell near the pool of Siloam killing eighteen people who were in the wrong place at the wrong time. The first was an intentionally evil act, the second purely accidental. Yet, how can such things be explained?

This is the quandary Jesus poses to a crowd of people. He asks the questions that were on people's minds. Were the Galileans worse sinners than other Galileans? Were the people killed by the tower worse offenders than others who came to wash in that pool? Did these people do something that made them deserving of punishment? Or, was God's will such that these awful things were intended to send a message to others?

Jesus answers his own question by saying this: "No, I tell you, but unless you repent, you will all perish as they did."

Jesus' words make our head spin! He seems to be contradicting himself.

Jesus is saying this: don't look for cause and effect explanations. Were those who died worse sinners? "No," he says, "but unless you repent, you will all perish as they did." Jesus is telling them to turn their attention toward their own lives --don't speculate about others.

What about our lives? We can spend so much energy trying to explain things --so much time fretting over other people's lives that we forget to pay attention to the reality of our own sin and need to turn toward God for mercy. Thus, Jesus says in so many words, "Let these senseless deaths awaken you. Repent."

You see, in answer to questions about cause and effect, why bad things happen to people--Jesus is not interested in our pursuit of answers. Jesus makes it clear that there is no rational explanation for these tragedies. He does not say, "It was God's will." The Galileans killed by Pilate were victims of an evil governor's whims. The people killed by the falling tower? It could have been anyone who happened to be standing there--just like the people who were seriously injured by flying parts when a race car slammed into the fence at Daytona International Speedway last weekend.

So, what does Jesus want to teach us through this story? Instead of providing answers to inexplicable suffering, tragedy and death, Jesus in so many words says "these trials and challenges should not stop you from following me and believing and trusting in a faithful, loving God. Repent." Repent is the word Jesus uses which involves a turning toward God. Repentance is a radical change in direction from a life lived for self, to a life lived under the mercy of God, and God's free and gracious acceptance of us.

Turn! Change! Go in the direction of God, is what Jesus teaches us in the face of unanswerable tragedy or loss. Instead of looking for answers that cannot be found, put your energy into faithfully following me, Jesus says.

Depending on what you want from God, this declaration by Jesus to repent, to turn, to quit worrying about why bad things happen--why tumors grow in our bodies and cars slide off rain slicked roads may not sound like good news. I doubt that it would have sounded like good news to the mother in that hospital waiting room. But for those of us who know how Jesus' life on this earth turned out; for those of us who have come to trust that God's will is for good, this is good news enough. In the fear of the world's crises, in response to the chaos that comes into our lives, what we can do is turn our faces to the cross and align our lives with God's mercy and God's will which we know chiefly in Jesus-- the Savior of the world. Amen.

Hope Amidst the Endings

Luke 21:25-36

'There will be signs in the sun, the moon, and the stars, and on the earth distress among nations confused by the roaring of the sea and the waves. People will faint from fear and foreboding of what is coming upon the world, for the powers of the heavens will be shaken. Then they will see "the Son of Man coming in a cloud" with power and great glory. Now when these things begin to take place, stand up and raise your heads, because your redemption is drawing near.'

Then he told them a parable: 'Look at the fig tree and all the trees; as soon as they sprout leaves you can see for yourselves and know that summer is already near. So also, when you see these things taking place, you know that the kingdom of God is near. Truly I tell you, this generation will not pass away until all things have taken place. Heaven and earth will pass away, but my words will not pass away.

'Be on guard so that your hearts are not weighed down with dissipation and drunkenness and the worries of this life, and that day does not catch you unexpectedly, like a trap. For it will come upon all who live on the face of the whole earth. Be alert at all times, praying that you may have the strength to escape all these things that will take place, and to stand before the Son of Man.'

Dear Sisters and Brothers in Christ:

I was visiting with a friend down in Texas recently and he was telling me how much the area has changed since I lived there several years ago. Gone are the quiet neighborhoods and the pastoral scenes of farm fields dotted with cattle and sheep. They have given way to huge real estate developments and ribbons of highways that link strip malls, hotels and corporate office buildings. Picturing all this as I visited with my friend brought back for me the memory of something shocking that I learned one winter down in Texas. When December rolled around, highway construction continued. It went on. In January, the bulldozers continued to cut into the earth. In February, concrete was being poured, covering the red soil. Highway construction never ended and neither did the accompanying frustration of traffic snarls caused by it.

It is good that some things and events come to an end. These words of Jesus tell us about an ending. So that got me to thinking about the endings we experience in life.

We experience endings all the time. Sometimes the endings are big, sometimes small. Often endings are simple, yet some are very complicated; endings can be joyful or sad. Some endings are happy:

- Endings of the semester and the school year;

- The end of mortgage or car payments;

- The end of kids in diapers.

Some endings bring a sense of accomplishment or maybe simply relief:

- End of college when the degree is achieved;

- End of your kid's soccer season;

- End of your working years.

Then, there are some endings which profoundly change our lives with considerable emotion:

- endings in our relationships and sometimes our marriages;

- endings of our parents' lives--and our spouse's, too;

- the end of the robust health or independent living.

Endings in our lives can provoke us and often dictate that we live life differently. In so many endings, there is not any choice in the matter.

However, some of the endings in our lives we can prepare for and anticipate. One of the best gifts for living that God has given us is the capacity to anticipate, to look forward to something:

- a game or party;

- a vacation or a trip;

- a visit from a friend;

- a reunion or anniversary.

To anticipate is to have a reason to set your heart and mind on the future. To anticipate future events is to be able to prepare for them, as well as the endings that come also. Our vacations will end. The friend will go back home. The anniversary will pass.

Future events often bring an array of experiences and emotions. We may wonder about retirement or what life will be like when the kids leave home. How we choose to view future events is solely our own doing. However, how we anticipate the future and the endings which come can significantly impact how we live today.

This Bible reading from Luke is about anticipating an ending--the end of the world--the rapture, the second-coming of Jesus. The basic theme in this season of Advent is anticipating the coming of Jesus at the end of time.

About that ending, Jesus says there will be *"distress among nations confused by the roaring of the sea and the waves. People will faint from fear and foreboding of what is coming upon the world."*

Jesus puts before us two options when it comes to choosing how we anticipate an ending and the end of time:

1. We can be fearful and worried, or

2. We can be faithful and vigilant.

When it comes to the end of the world, Jesus says *"Look for the signs. There will be distress among nations."*

Well, we already know that, don't we? Today, Americans are a fearful lot. We have been fed fear daily by our nation's leaders. We see and hear fear every time we look at TV or listen to the radio. Today, we are fearful about terrorism and violence, contamination of our food supply and ground water. We are fearful about Avian flu and new strains of micro-organisms and the waning ability of antibiotics to fight them. An increasing number of scientific experts and ordinary people like me are concerned about climate change or global warming, melting ice caps, vast droughts, and the general demise of the environment. We rightly have sizeable concern about nuclear proliferation. There is no shortage of fear as we anticipate the future.

But to all this worry and fear about signs of the end, Jesus says *"Now when these things begin to take place, stand up and raise your heads, because your redemption is drawing near."*

When it comes to worry and concern about the present or the future, about your life, your family, your health or your standing with God, Jesus says, do not worry! He must have said it a dozen times in a dozen ways. Jesus said: *"Do not worry about your life, what you will eat or what you will drink, what you will wear"* (Mt 6:25). *"Do not be afraid, for it is your Father's good pleasure to give you the kingdom"* (Lk 12:32). *"Can any of you by worrying add a single hour to your life?"* (Luke 12:25). In Philippians (4:6) it says, *"Don't worry about anything, but pray about everything."*

Instead of fear for the future, Jesus says, *"Be on guard so that your hearts are not weighed down...with the worries of this life, and that day catch you unexpectedly."*

Jesus always has marching orders for us. He wants us to be vigilant in our living because there still are things that tempt us and attempt to drive us from God. So, Jesus tells us to keep on our toes, stay awake, keep watch!

Our lives as faithful people must involve vigilance. There is so much fear around and so many temptations that waft about seeking to divert us from faithful choices. So, Jesus says, *"Be on guard so that the endings in life don't catch you by surprise and unprepared."*

The good news is that God has already provided us with the means for being on guard while we live our days. So, my friends, here are some options for vigilant faithfulness as you go about your daily lives:

- Pray and worship. God has given us Word of life and hope and feeds us with the riches of the Lord's supper where we can reconnect with God and the forgiving, merciful love so lavishly and freely shared with us.

- Stand together with fellow believers. God has provided us with the communion of saints--each other, so that our lives are supported and encouraged by fellow believers.

- Serve and share. God has directed us to serve our neighbor and share our wealth, so that we do not get too focused on our own concerns and lose all perspective.

My friends, in the endings you experience in life, and until that ending day when the Lord comes again, the Church will be here so that our lives might be guided, our thoughts and actions directed, and our hope sustained through Jesus Christ our Lord. Amen.

Just for Good

Jeremiah 31:31-34

The days are surely coming, says the Lord, when I will make a new covenant with the house of Israel and the house of Judah. It will not be like the covenant that I made with their ancestors when I took them by the hand to bring them out of the land of Egypt—a covenant that they broke, though I was their husband, says the Lord. But this is the covenant that I will make with the house of Israel after those days, says the Lord: I will put my law within them, and I will write it on their hearts; and I will be their God, and they shall be my people. No longer shall they teach one another, or say to each other, 'Know the Lord', for they shall all know me, from the least of them to the greatest, says the Lord; for I will forgive their iniquity, and remember their sin no more.

Dear Friends:

When I was a kid, there was a gas station in town that gave away beach balls every summer. If you filled up your tank, you got a beach ball for free. Few people took the offer. Then one summer the station started selling the balls for $.49 cents each. Sales were brisk. The owner of the gas station, when asked about this said this "At $.49 cents people figured the beach balls were a bargain. But when they were free, people figured they were cheap and worthless, and were not interested in them."

Often, we think that way. If something is free, if you do not have to pay a price, then it is probably not worth too much. Perhaps you know the clichés about free things. *"You get what you pay for"* or *"If it sounds too good to be true (because it's free) it probably is too good to be true."*

Well, this situation of getting something for free and thinking that it is not worth much also happened in Biblical times. The Old Testament is filled with accounts of God doing good things for people, simply out of God's heart of love.

In the Bible reading today from the book of Jeremiah we are reminded of God's heart. In it are the wonderful words about a new covenant, a new promise God will make with people. In Jeremiah, God says *"I will be their God, and they shall be my people...I will forgive them and remember their sin no more."*

The Bible reading announces God's plan. It's a plan that creates a new way for God to be in relationship with people, even when they're unfaithful to God. It comes after the people of Israel had broken the covenant God made with Moses. That covenant was laid out in the 10 commandments. The people had failed miserably in keeping those commandments. Yet, God continued to be their God. God didn't decide to start charging the people in hopes they would realize what a good thing was being given to them. Just the opposite is what Jeremiah announces on behalf of God. What he says is that God is going to initiate a new covenant, a new promise for people that cannot be broken by human unfaithfulness.

That new covenant would be revealed in Jesus. It would give us a clear way of understanding the truth that God's very nature is to love and to forgive people. You do not have to pay a price. God takes care of that for you.

Some years ago during a sabbatical, I volunteered to teach English in a middle school in Barlad, Romania. During the weekend, a few of the American volunteers took a side-trip into the Moldavia region where we visited the famous painted monasteries. On Sunday morning we were in the eastern Romanian city of Iasi and went to worship at a Russian Orthodox Church. It was the season of Lent and the Russian Orthodox people were remembering the story of St. Mary of Egypt. The legend is that back in the 400's, there was a woman of ill repute who lived in Egypt by the name of Mary. She was known widely for leading a very sinful life. In hopes of landing for herself more business, she joined a group on a pilgrimage to Jerusalem for a religious festival. Just as the group was about to enter the church in Jerusalem believed to be at the site of where Jesus was buried, Mary was stopped.

The legend is told that as Mary neared the entrance of the church, she felt as if there was a hand in front of her, stopping her from going in. It was at that point that Mary came to realize how her sin was keeping her away from God. Mary's life turned completely from that experience.

Soon after, Mary learned of this new covenant that Jeremiah announces. It made all the difference. Mary began to learn of a God who loved her and provided forgiveness. The legend ends explaining that Mary dedicated the remaining 40 years of her life believing in God's love in Jesus and living the kind of life that Jesus wanted her to live.

Jeremiah's word is good news for you and me too. Here we are reminded that God's love and forgiveness is not something that we can go out and earn for ourselves. But often our minds trick us into thinking the opposite. We think that if we do the right things and say the right words, or follow the church's laws to the letter, then God will have to forgive us. But that is not the way God works. You see, it is not that we need to find some way to climb our way up to God. We cannot buy God's favor. Instead, Jeremiah reminds us that God reaches out to us and lifts us up. "I will be their God, and they shall be my people."

The gift of God's saving love and forgiveness is not our work. It is God's work. In other words, saving us is something that God wants to do. It is not something that we need to go out and do for ourselves.

Do you like having the opportunity for a new start? When you have not succeeded in some endeavor, do you appreciate getting a second chance? Well, Jeremiah tell us that God says; *"I am making a new start possible and you cannot fail me this time."* God says: *"I will make a new covenant...and I will write it on people's hearts."*

For us as Christians this new covenant is made known in Jesus, who on that evening before his crucifixion, when he sat down for supper with his disciples, shared the wine and said: *"This is the new covenant in my blood, shed for you and for all people for the forgiveness of sins."* Jesus is the new covenant, God's promise to us that God forgives us and saves us. Because of Jesus we get a new promise of God's love and it doesn't cost you a thing. God pays the price out of that amazing love that is the heart of God.

So, where does this good news leave us in the living of these days? Now that we do not have to earn God's love and forgiveness, what then shall we do with this faith in God?

Well, this good news leaves us with a mission. The mission is to freely share this love and forgiveness given to us by God. I hope you carry out this mission in your life every day!

Coming together in worship is part of the mission. It is necessary that we gather with one another to thank and praise God for this unmerited favor. Then it is imperative that we are sent out to live this goodness each day. We don't carry out this mission as a way of paying back God. We engage in the mission of sharing and serving in Christ's love because God's new covenant has been written on our hearts.

For many years I offered people of the church I served opportunities to engage in hands-on mission projects in

Jamaica as an expression of their love for God. One March we were in Kingston building a simple 12'x 20' house for an older man who lived alone. Located in an area of the city where rusted metal and scrap wood form most of the ramshackle houses in which people live, it's a tough place. Despair, poverty, violence and a meager way of life is the rule of the neighborhood.

As we were busy building one morning, a carload of heavily armed police officers pulled up in front of our project site. I went over and introduced myself and explained we were Americans from a Lutheran Church in the USA, and that we were working in cooperation with Maranatha Church a few blocks away. I went on to explain that our mission was one of serving and sharing our faith in the hope that we might make life better for others.

The police officer was a bit confused as he marveled over all these white people sawing and drilling and painting behind me. He asked: "Why are you doing this?" I explained again. And then he said with a notable inflection of surprise "You are doing this just for good?"

"Yup, just for good" I replied.

May the new covenant of God's good love and forgiveness for you bring you renewed hope for life and the living out of the mission of sharing the gift of God's grace in Christ. Amen.

More than the Details

Christmas Eve
Luke 2: 1-16
In those days a decree went out from Emperor Augustus that all the world should be registered. This was the first registration and was taken while Quirinius was governor of Syria. All went to their own towns to be registered. Joseph also went from the town of Nazareth in Galilee to Judea, to the city of David called Bethlehem, because he was descended from the house and family of David. He went to be registered with Mary, to whom he was engaged and who was expecting a child. While they were there, the time came for her to deliver her child. And she gave birth to her firstborn son and wrapped him in bands of cloth, and laid him in a manger, because there was no place for them in the inn.

In that region there were shepherds living in the fields, keeping watch over their flock by night. Then an angel of the Lord stood before them, and the glory of the Lord shone around them, and they were terrified. But the angel said to them, "Do not be afraid; for see—I am bringing you good news of great joy for all the people: to you is born this day in the city of David a Savior, who is the Messiah, the Lord. This will be a sign for you: you will find a child wrapped in bands of cloth and lying in a manger." And suddenly there was with the angel a multitude of the heavenly host, praising God and saying, "Glory to God in the highest heaven, and on earth peace among those whom he favors!" When the angels had left them and gone into heaven, the shepherds said to one another, "Let us go now to Bethlehem and see this thing that has taken place, which the Lord has made known to us." So, they went with haste and found Mary and Joseph, and the child lying in the manger.

Christmas Eve

Dear Sisters and Brothers, may the wonder and hope of God, come to us in the birth of Jesus, be good news for you always. Amen.

One fall in the church I served, we began an eight month walk through the Bible using the book **The Story** by Randy Frazee and Max Lucado. It is an abridged, chronological Bible that reads like a novel. For people intimidated or overwhelmed by the unabridged Bible, **The Story** helps readers understand God's Word more fully and engage with it more easily.

Our lives are comprised of stories. Our stories have lots of details, some insignificant and some which are key to who we are. When we tell our stories, there are usually some details that we can't leave out. Whether it's the weight and length of your child upon birth, or what church you were married in or how old you were when your dad died, or the layout of the hole where you shot that hole in one, there are details that are important to the stories of our lives.

The Bible contains an Upper Story and a Lower Story. The Upper Story tells the big picture, the grand narrative of

God seeking to be in relationship with humankind as it unfolds throughout history. The Lower Story contains the details of particular people, like Adam and Eve, Moses, Noah, Mary, Peter and others. The Lower Story helps us better understand the Upper Story, which becomes for us a framework around which we approach and apply the Bible to our story. The Upper Story helps guide us through the hard times of our own Lower Story by reminding us of God's eternal, long-range plan. Knowing of that grace, we then can put our experiences into a divine context formed by a loving God.

For example, without the Upper Story, a lost job could be an event without hope. But put into the context of the larger chronicle of our lives, and God's loving intention, that lost job can be seen in a very different light, perhaps as an opportunity for God to reveal something better.

The story of God that draws us together on Christmas Eve has many details of Upper and Lower story. There are details about an angel and its dramatic announcement to shepherds who were doing their work out in the countryside. There is detail in learning the shepherds were curious and hurried to check out this news of a birth.

This story of Christmas would be important without all the details, because the truth of the story is still the same: God loved this world so much, that God became one of us, so that we might know that God is *for us* and wants us to love one another.

But back to the details of this biblical story of Jesus' birth. I've wondered about the details told us regarding "no room in the inn."

Do you think that's true? Maybe the innkeeper had a room left, but he saw this unmarried couple, the woman obviously very pregnant, and decided he didn't approve. So, he told them there was no room available.

Shortly before Christmas I traveled with a group to Bethlehem and the Church of the Nativity, which is said to be the place where Jesus was born and laid in a manger. This spot is considered so holy, that three Christian traditions: Roman Catholic, Greek Orthodox and Armenian have laid claim to it for centuries.

Each of the traditions have priests and monks that live on this spot in an uneasy truce. It is not uncommon that these holy men feud over the place. They accuse the other of encroaching on parts of the church to which they lay claim. Four years ago, the annual cleaning of this church deteriorated into a brawl between rival priests and monks battling each other with brooms until police intervened.

Having been to Bethlehem twice, I must say it is enlightening, even as it presents a very different picture from all the Nativity scenes that are on display this holiday. The church that has been built over the supposed spot of Jesus' birth isn't impressive. It would never existed if the Innkeeper had opened a room for Mary and Joseph. I wonder if the owner ever realized who he turned away that night. Details, details.

The birthday of Jesus that brings billions of people into churches across the world isn't about what an innkeeper did 2,000 years ago. It isn't about a spot where a young woman gave birth. It's about what God did, and what God still does. And it's about what we do next with out lives in the context of the Upper Story.

My friends, Christmas is not simply about recalling the story with all its details. Likewise, all the activity that marks the season, the shopping, decorating, food preparation, traveling, and gathering has to be about more than just an event that happened centuries ago.

For Christmas to have any lasting value in our lives, this story we love to hear and sing about must teach us about opening ourselves to God. I think God is waiting for us to get to the important detail intended for us in the coming of Jesus in Bethlehem. And when we get to that detail in our lives, then the world has a chance for some hope.

It's been a rough year here on planet Earth: One million people have fled their home countries trying to find a safe land in which to live; terror groups took to beheading people and recording it for everyone to see; evil people with enormous guns or bombs strapped to their bodies have carried out mass killings in places where life is usually innocent and safe. Add to the long list of horrors, religions being misaligned by extremists who misrepresent timeless, loving truths about God, and I suspect we all could use a good measure of hope that the next year will be better. I must believe that God hopes the same. But that brings me back to the details and you and me.

The important detail that God wishes to be the core of your life starts at Christmas, in the birth of a Savior.

After Jesus grew up, he was asked what God wants of people. He answered: *Love the Lord your God with all your heart and love your neighbor as yourself. (Luke 10:27)* In other words, the detail focuses on what we do with love.

When the Christmas dinner has been eaten, the gifts opened, when the relatives go home; when the tree comes down and the nativity set goes back into the box, what remains? That is the ultimate test of the details of the Christmas celebration. I suspect the success or failure of that test will be in how well we open our hearts to that detail of love born at Christmas and shared for all.

Nit-Pickers and Arm-Wavers

John 9:13-17, 34-39
They brought to the Pharisees the man who had formerly been blind. Now it was a sabbath day when Jesus made the mud and opened his eyes. Then the Pharisees also began to ask him how he had received his sight. He said to them, 'He put mud on my eyes. Then I washed, and now I see.' Some of the Pharisees said, 'This man is not from God, for he does not observe the sabbath.' But others said, 'How can a man who is a sinner perform such signs?' And they were divided. So, they said again to the blind man, 'What do you say about him? It was your eyes he opened.' He said, 'He is a prophet.' They answered him, 'You were born entirely in sins, and are you trying to teach us?' And they drove him out.
Jesus heard that they had driven him out, and when he found him, he said, 'Do you believe in the Son of Man?' He answered, 'And who is he, sir? Tell me, so that I may believe in him.' Jesus said to him, 'You have seen him, and the one speaking with you is he.' He said, 'Lord, I believe.' And he worshipped him. Jesus said, 'I came into this world for judgement so that those who do not see may see, and those who do see may become blind.'

Dear Friends:

There is much speculation about the idiom, "Here's mud in your eye!" Google the sentence and you will find 1.6 million hits to explain its origin and meaning. Some attribute it to the world of horse racing where the winning horse will kick mud into the eyes of those following. The phrase was bandied about in saloons as early as 1890. Farmers would raise a glass to the success of a good harvest: "Here's mud in your eye!"

Then there are those who say the origin of this phrase is Biblical. It refers to the story of Jesus and the blind man you just heard. They say it came from the unusual story in which Jesus spat in the dirt and made mud and rubbed it onto the eyes of a blind man and healed the man's sight after telling him to go wash it off in the Pool of Siloam. I'm going to choose to go with this helpful, positive origin for the phrase, "here's mud in your eye."

One day Jesus came upon a man blind since birth. This was not unusual. Needy people would frequently position themselves in public places and, if possible, near the entrance to the Temple hoping that passersby would be in a charitable mode.

As Jesus and his disciples came upon a blind man, they asked Jesus, *"Rabbi, who sinned, this man or his parents, that he was born blind?"*

We commonly ask questions of "why." Why is the man blind? When we learn of something bad happening, we want to know why. Quickly our attention is diverted from the need at hand. So, it was with the disciples.

"Who sinned, this man or his parents, that he was born blind?" they asked. It is also human nature to try and find cause or blame. Why is there blindness in the world? Who

is to blame for this man's blindness, nature or nurture--this man or his parents?"

Jesus, as he so often does, answers with a third option, one that escaped his questioners. Jesus said, *"Neither this man sinned, nor his parents. This man is here, before us blind, so that the marvelous works of God can be shown."* Jesus sees opportunity, a chance to recognize God's work in an act which pays close attention to the need itself.

In the Bible story about Jesus today, we also meet some interesting characters who hold a decidedly negative view of Jesus. They are the Pharisees. The Pharisees were educated, religious people of the day who followed every letter of religious law. In this story, the Pharisees were doing their best to see all the negatives in Jesus' action of giving the blind man sight.

The whole scenario starts as Jesus and the disciples are walking along and encounter the blind man. True to his style, Jesus desired to do something to help the man and to reveal himself as God's son. So, using a mixture of mud and spit, Jesus made a mud pack--then tells the man to go and wash it off. He is not present when the man finally gets to see for the first time in his life.

None of this goes unnoticed by the Pharisees. It did not take them long to question the healed man about what happened. They wanted to know if he had really been blind? Maybe this was all a fraud and the guy was playing along to make Jesus look good. The Pharisees sought out the man's parents in hopes of finding some technicalities to discount Jesus' miracle. In the end the Pharisees were divided in their response to the miracle. Some of them were convinced that Jesus was a dangerous fraud. Others were still uncertain.

The climax of the story comes when Jesus speaks to the healed man after he had been interrogated by the Pharisees. In that conversation, Jesus reveals that he is the Son of God. At that point everything changes because the man believes. This prompts the once-blind man to worship Jesus.

As I think about this story, I'm amazed at how the people who witnessed this miracle responded so negatively. The Pharisees, considering a stupendous event sought only to see the negative. I call them nitpickers.

Ever met a nitpicker? Nit-pickers are people who can burst any bubble. They are great at throwing a wet towel on the best events. They are skilled at jabbing people in the stomach and the heart. Nit-pickers say things like:

- Congratulations on your promotion. But you've still got an awful lot of the ladder to climb, don't you?

- The service was nice pastor, but the music was too loud.

- The wedding was so beautiful; such a shame the bride couldn't have lost a few pounds for the occasion.

Deflating joy, tarnishing triumphs, criticizing, that's what nitpickers do best.

- It is a wonderful thing that a blind man got healed, but it is awful that Jesus did it on the Sabbath.

You see how the nitpicking kills the joy of a great happening in a man's life and everyone misses seeing the goodness of the Gentle Healer.

Three persons arrived at the Pearly Gates at the same time. St. Peter greeted them but said he had some pressing business and asked if they would please wait. St. Peter left and was gone a long time, but finally returned and called one of the new arrivals in and asked if she had minded waiting.

"No" she said, "I've looked forward to this for so long. I love God and I can't wait to meet Jesus. I don't mind at all."

St. Peter then said, "Well, I have one more question. How do you spell God?"

She said, "Capital G-o-d."

St. Peter said, "Go right in."

Next St. Peter went outside and got another new arrival, told him to come on inside, and said, "Did you mind waiting?"

The man said, "Oh, no. I've been a Christian for 80 years and I'll spend eternity here. I didn't mind waiting."

So, St. Peter said, "Just one more thing. How do you spell God?"

He said, "G-o-d. No, I mean capital G."

St. Peter said that was good and sent him into heaven.

St. Peter went back out and invited the third person in and asked him if he had minded waiting.

"As a matter of fact, I did," he replied. "I've had to wait in line all my life, at the supermarket, at school, at stop lights, everywhere and now I resent having to wait in line for heaven!"

St. Peter said, "Well, that's all right for you to feel that way. It won't be held against you, but there is just one more question. How do you spell Kazakhstan?"

Nit-pickers.

Jesus' healing of the blind man gives us opportunity to ask ourselves: "Do we see the good that God provides in life or do we dwell in the negative, the nitpicky?

What I really like about this Bible story is how Jesus and the blind man rescue us from the nitpickers. It comes at the end when something remarkable and wonderful happens. The healed man comes to believe Jesus is the Son of God and he then worships Jesus. This man is not a nitpicker. I call him an arm-waver.

Some of you are arm-wavers. Arm-wavers are people who celebrate victories and lend support in times of defeat. Arm-wavers hoot and holler when their child's Little League team wins the game -- but they also cheer and give great hugs when the team loses 10 in a row. It's not that the arm-wavers don't see imperfections, but they choose to not focus on them. Take that hand-knit sweater from Aunt Tootie who is a lousy knitter. The nitpicker sees the flaws and the arm-waver focuses on all the beauty that surrounds the flaws.

Thinking about this Bible story, it's amazing that the arm-wavers were absent for so long. Here is a stunning miracle -- a man born blind suddenly given sight--and no one celebrates. No one says, "Wow, that was great! How wonderful, my friend, that you can see." Or "Do it again Jesus! Thanks, good work!" Instead, everyone looks at the negative. The healed man's neighbors were doubtful; his parents were worried about the religious officials and how they were going to respond; while the Pharisees found the whole event threatening. Not until the healed man himself finally realizes who Jesus is and what his presence means, do we get the first sign of arm-waving.

Erma Bombeck was a humorist who died too young. I always read her stories in the newspaper. One of her favorite stories was about a grandmother who took her grandson to the beach one day, complete with bucket, shovel and sun hat. While the boy played in the sand, grandma dozed off. As she slept, a large wave rolled in and dragged the child out to sea. When the grandmother awoke and could not located her grandson, she was devastated. She fell to the ground on her knees and prayed, "God, if you save my grandchild, I promise I will make it up to you. I will go to church every week, volunteer at the hospital, give to the poor and do anything that makes you happy."

Suddenly, another huge wave rolled in and tossed her grandson on the beach right at her feet. She quickly kneeled and noticed color in his cheeks. His eyes were bright. He was alive! As the grandmother stood up, however, she seemed to be upset. She put her hands on her hips, looked skyward, and said sharply, "He had a hat on, you know."

Deflating or ignoring joy is what nitpickers, negative people are good at. They are always noting what is wrong with something or someone rather than what is good, what is encouraging or simply right. Nit-picking, negative people cannot enjoy much in life. The nitpickers in this Bible story are the Pharisees. Instead of rejoicing with the man at the miracle of sight, they can only focus on the possible infringements on the religious law.

So, who are you? Are you the arm-waver or the nitpicker? Where would you be in this Bible story?

We all have a great opportunity and it's a calling as Christians to look for the good and to encourage one another. As a congregation moving through transition, soon you will be welcoming a new pastor. Ahead are challenges. How will you change to reach younger generations? Amidst the challenges, there is opportunity galore. But where will you stand? Will you be a nitpicker? Or will you be arm-wavers able to see the goodness of God providing and leading you forward?

Like the friends, neighbors, family and Pharisees around the man healed of blindness, we can focus on the negative--we can be fearful of challenge--or suspect of others--or unwilling to appreciate what God is providing. In short, we can be the nitpickers just like those Pharisees and the neighbors of the blind man.

But I think there's a better way. A faithful way. A holy way. Many times, our individual words of praise or thanks, encouragement or cheer have moved people to greater faith and engaged them in a thankful way of life. And from that lives are transformed and the ways of Christ advanced through us. Blessed are those who speak such a word. Amen.

On Wonder

Matthew 2:1-9
In the time of King Herod, after Jesus was born in Bethlehem of Judea, wise men from the East came to Jerusalem, asking, 'Where is the child who has been born king of the Jews? For we observed his star at its rising and have come to pay him homage.' When King Herod heard this, he was frightened, and all Jerusalem with him; and calling together all the chief priests and scribes of the people, he inquired of them where the Messiah was to be born. They told him, 'In Bethlehem of Judea; for so it has been written by the prophet:
"And you, Bethlehem, in the land of Judah, are by no means least among the rulers of Judah;
for from you shall come a ruler who is to shepherd my people Israel."'
Then Herod secretly called for the wise men and learned from them the exact time when the star had appeared. Then he sent them to Bethlehem, saying, 'Go and search diligently for the child; and when you have found him, bring me word so that I may also go and pay him homage.' When they had heard the king, they set out; and there, ahead of them, went the star that they had seen at its rising, until it stopped over the place where the child was.

Dear Sisters and Brothers, may the brightness of the Bethlehem star, the curiosity of the wise men and the grace of the One born Prince of Peace be with you always.

Ten days ago, a record number of people came to this place of worship filled with the warmth and anticipation of Christmas. Candles flickered, the poinsettias were red and fresh, families smiled, the music was heavenly, and the children looked like angels. It was a glorious celebration of Christmas. The best.

But it has been over a week since Christmas eve and some of you are happy to be tossing out the tree, packing up the decorations and moving along into a new season. Most people I listened to this week admitted they're happy that Christmas came and went.

The Bible reading this day does not let us push along the calendar too quickly and leave Christmas behind so fast. Today's reading is about the Epiphany, which in a quainter time in American society marked the end of the 12 days of Christmas.

Epiphany means "appearance" and celebrates the encounter of the Wise Men and Jesus. It is a story that snags our imagination and draws us back to a sense of wonder that marked our lives and the holiday 10 days ago. I hope this story might inspire some of the same feelings that marked the recent Christmas and provide you a sense of wonder for God.

Some quick history about the wise men. Their business was to read the sky - so upon the birth of Jesus they noticed a new star appeared. In the first century world, stars were believed to announce the birth of important people, usually royalty. So, when the wise men saw this new star, it prompted many questions: "What new significant leader has been born? To what royal family? Where was he born? What kind of new king will he be? The wise men could not answer those questions.

So, they followed the new star which led them to Jerusalem. There they checked in with a king named Herod. They thought he should know if a new royal family member had been born. Herod was a mean and selfish king and this curiosity of the wise men made him very nervous. If a new king had been born – it could mean trouble for Herod. So, Herod, ever the conniving guy, told the wise men to follow the star and when they found the one they were looking for, to come back and report, so that he too, could go and worship the newborn king. But Herod wasn't telling the truth-- what he really wanted to do was to destroy this baby born to be king. He wanted no rival to his throne.

Well, the wise men left Herod and followed the night star to Bethlehem. The Bible tells us "When they saw that the star had stopped, they were overwhelmed with joy." (Matthew 2:10). Then, inside a house they found the baby and his parents, and they worshiped him.

The wise men brought gifts of precious minerals to the baby, but I am thinking they brought another kind of gift that was very precious, a gift of far more value than gold, frankincense and myrrh. The wise men brought the gift of wonder. It was wonder that motived them in the first place.

Have you thought about where in your life is a sense of wonder? This story prompts me to view wonder as a gift to inspire our faithful living. Wonder, it motivated those wise men to find the new born King and worship him. Wonder, it can motivate us to reach toward the future God unfolds. Wonder, it can fuel us with faith, hope and love for the living of our days.

How is your sense of wonder these days? Famous poet D.H. Lawrence called wonder the most precious element in life, he named it our sixth sense. "When all comes to all, the most precious element in life is wonder. Love is a great emotion, and power is power, but both love and power are based on wonder."

Thinking about the people in this Bible story we see that:

- King Herod went for power;

- Joseph and Mary might have said the most important element in life is love;

- But the wise men teach us that to be able to get on that road toward the sacred, we need a sense of wonder.

Wonder holds gratitude and awe together. Wonder is the ability to be caught off guard and startled by the beauty, the power, the awesome nature of God. The philosopher Aristotle said that philosophy, the ability to ask questions about the world, begins with a sense of wonder. So, does spirituality and our faith in God.

Czeslaw Milosz, was a Polish poet, Nobel prize winner and professor at UC Berkeley. He lived in Warsaw during the Nazi occupation. He survived many tragedies in his life. But wonder did something for him amid many great trials. He wrote that life is pure beauty and blessing and that even amid bitterness and confusion "Wonder kept dazzling me and I recall only wonder." He found wonder in the world around him to inspire his faith and awareness of God. "Wonder keeps dazzling me!" How often does wonder dazzle you during challenges?

Wonder inspired the wise men to find baby Jesus, to give gifts and to worship him. They were dazzled with the wonder of God come to earth. They were dazzled by the wonder of God providing a sacred pathway to something better.

Have you been dazzled with wonder this Christmas - over the truth that God has come to earth? How might wonder inspire your faithful living this year? I believe the wonder of God in this new year can transform the ordinariness of life and provide for us a sacred pathway to something better, too.

The new year begins and the Christian church serves up the wise men to us to remind us to see the wonder of God. I hope you'll sense wonder over the truth of God's love for you; Wonder over the amazing grace that you are forgiven in Christ; Wonder over the promise from Jesus that there is a place prepared for you when life on this earth is done.

So, my friends - GO! Go with wonder into the new year ahead. Go into each day with wonder. May your daily living let the whole world know the wonder of life in God. Amen.

One Thing Jesus Cannot Do

Luke 13: 31-35
At that very hour some Pharisees came and said to him,
'Get away from here, for Herod wants to kill you.' He said
to them, 'Go and tell that fox for me, "Listen, I am casting
out demons and performing cures today and tomorrow, and
on the third day I finish my work. Yet today, tomorrow, and
the next day I must be on my way, because it is impossible
for a prophet to be killed away from Jerusalem."
Jerusalem, Jerusalem, the city that kills the prophets and
stones those who are sent to it! How often have I desired to
gather your children together as a hen gathers her brood
under her wings, and you were not willing! See, your house
is left to you. And I tell you, you will not see me until the
time comes when you say, "Blessed is the one who comes in
the name of the Lord."'

Dear Friends:

In the movie, *Ulee's Gold*, Peter Fonda plays an older man who makes a living by producing and selling honey. It is exhausting work and Ulee does most of it by himself because he cannot afford to hire help. With precise dedication, Ulee maintains the hives, gathers the trays, separates the honey from the wax, spins the final product into jars, and ships it off to market. At night when he cannot sleep, Ulee worries about the constant changes in the price of honey. As the movie goes along you can almost watch the spirit drain out of Ulee.

Beyond bee keeping, what really weighs on Ulee is his daughter. She is an absent mother, addicted to drugs and living in a treatment center. Unable to care for her two girls, Ulee is raising them alone since the death of his wife.

The oldest granddaughter is a teenager. Her life has been keenly impacted by her mother's addiction and absence. She is dating a guy who is older than her and Ulee is trying to keep a tight rein on this teenager. He remembers his own daughter's rebellion during the teenage years, and he is intent to lay down the parameters with this granddaughter. Like any good parent, he has a curfew in effect, though it doesn't work very well. Ulee is insistent this teen is going to follow his rules. "You just try to figure out a way to make me" she yells at her grandfather.

For any of you who have raised children and for all of us who are kids or once were, these words are familiar to us, aren't they? "You just try to make me." I know I used them.

In this scripture passage Jesus is dealing with big concerns for people he has loved and cared for who challenge and reject him. You can almost hear the people of Israel saying to Jesus, "You just try to make me love you."

One of the popular images of Jesus is that he can do anything. Walk on water. Turn a couple fish and a few loaves of bread into a feast for thousands. Jesus can make the deaf hear, the paralyzed walk. He can even raise the dead. Throughout the ages you can just hear people saying: "That's our Jesus, he can do anything."

This Biblical scene brings that popular image of Jesus to a screeching halt. Jesus can do many impressive things. But there is one thing Jesus cannot do. Jesus cannot make people love him. No matter how passionate or deeply He loves people, Jesus cannot persuade, coax, woo, or coerce people into loving Him.

In a rather sad picture of Jesus, we hear him saying: *"Oh, you people-- how often have I desired to gather you together, and you were not willing."* Jesus cannot do anything to get the people to respond to his love.

In the movie, Ulee knew the feeling Jesus' expresses. Jesus can do a lot of amazing things. But he can only watch as his children leave the dinner table and go through the screen door saying, "You just try to figure out a way to make me love you."

To love and not be loved in return is tough to experience. Has your love ever been unreturned? We can do all kinds of crazy, zany things to get someone's attention and love. It seems that Jesus is willing to make a fool of himself to get our attention, too.

In this passage we see how. Jesus likens himself to a hen. To a chicken. Out of all the animals that Jesus could have chosen, he chooses a chicken.[2] Don't you just want to shake your head and say, "Really Jesus, if you love us and want to care for us, what kind of confidence does likening yourself to a chicken instill in us?" We need a better image than that!" In this crazy world, wouldn't you prefer to think of Jesus the hovering eagle or the prowling lion at your side rather than Jesus the mother hen?

But no, Jesus likens himself to a chicken. And I wonder, if Jesus cannot get people to love him in return what chance does Jesus the mother hen have against all the things that distract us from loving God? Can Jesus the chicken deal with this troubled, sinful world in which we live?

Well, as the story of Jesus goes on, we find out the forces of evil that lurked eventually caught up with Jesus, the mother hen. It's the world we still live in, isn't it? Evil continues to have an allure, wooing away the hearts of God's brood.

But back to the Bible reading. Here is the troubling thing: Jesus is powerless to stop it. He can walk on water and raise the dead, but he cannot make us love him. He desires such love, but he cannot force it. Jesus cannot keep us from slamming the screen door in his face, defenseless against the many evils waiting to sweep us up.

---

[2] "As a Hen Gathers Her Brood" The Christian Century (February 25, 1986), p. 201.

One of the hardest things in life is loving someone you know you can't shelter or protect.

So, what is Jesus' plan? What is he going to do now? In our time, some preachers and some churches have turned to using fear and lots of rules and laws to get people to love Jesus. They have guilted and threatened people with pronouncements that they will go to hell if they do not love God.

Strangely, God's plan is to have Jesus continually offer the love of a mother hen. He keeps spreading his wings. As we already know, he will offer his life to Herod on our behalf. He will follow us into the darkness we have chosen for ourselves, repeatedly. He will love us when we do not love him. He will grieve with us when we are hurt by people who do not love us back. He will cry with us when our hearts are broken. Jesus will place himself between the forces of evil and us. And if you look closely at this man hanging on the cross, his arms outstretched, the span of his reach on that wood will begin to resemble the loving wings of a mother hen, gathering up her chicks in a love that does not make sense.

Jesus does not count on the world ever understanding such love. And even as he hangs there nailed to a tree, he cannot make us love him. Jesus cannot make us receive or return his love. But his desire for us is there. Always, eternally there. *"How often have I desired to gather your children together as a hen gathers her brood under her wings, and you were not willing."*

While these are ancient words, they are timeless. To you. To this conflicted world. To the person who has not returned your love or has broken your heart. These are timeless words for the people you wish were sitting next to you today, but they are not, because they just do not care that much about Jesus.

Jesus was a powerful teacher. A worker of miracles. A preacher who shook this world to its foundations. But guess what? I have decided that he is not all-powerful. That may sound shocking, but he is not. There is one little thing that Jesus needs of you. One thing that he desires but cannot (or will not) control. He desires your will. Your independent, self-sufficient, proud control over your destiny. To relinquish that is both the hardest and the sweetest thing we will ever do. Amen.

Out of Mysteriously Divine Love:
Black Box, Empty Tomb and Goo

Easter Sunday

John 20: 1-18

Early on the first day of the week, while it was still dark, Mary Magdalene came to the tomb and saw that the stone had been removed from the tomb. So, she ran and went to Simon Peter and the other disciple, the one whom Jesus loved, and said to them, 'They have taken the Lord out of the tomb, and we do not know where they have laid him.' Then Peter and the other disciple set out and went towards the tomb. The two were running together, but the other disciple outran Peter and reached the tomb first. He bent down to look in and saw the linen wrappings lying there, but he did not go in. Then Simon Peter came, following him, and went into the tomb. He saw the linen wrappings lying there, and the cloth that had been on Jesus' head, not lying with the linen wrappings but rolled up in a place by itself. Then the other disciple, who reached the tomb first, also went in, and he saw and believed; for as yet they did not understand the scripture, that he must rise from the dead. Then the disciples returned to their homes.

But Mary stood weeping outside the tomb. As she wept, she bent over to look into the tomb; and she saw two angels in white, sitting where the body of Jesus had been lying, one at the head and the other at the feet. They said to her, 'Woman, why are you weeping?' She said to them, 'They have taken away my Lord, and I do not know where they have laid him.' When she had said this, she turned around and saw Jesus standing there, but she did not know that it was Jesus. Jesus said to her, 'Woman, why are you weeping? For whom are you looking?' Supposing him to be the gardener, she said to him, 'Sir, if you have carried him away, tell me where you have laid him, and I will take him away.' Jesus said to her, 'Mary!' She turned and said to him in Hebrew, 'Rabbouni!' (which means Teacher). Jesus said to her, 'Do not hold on to me, because I have not yet ascended to the Father. But go to my brothers and say to them, "I am ascending to my Father and your Father, to my God and your God."' Mary Magdalene went and announced to the disciples, 'I have seen the Lord'; and she told them that he had said these things to her.[3]

Dear Friends, on this day of resurrection, may the life, hope and goodness of God in Christ be yours in abundance.

Today, Christians across the globe celebrate this news of resurrection--about Jesus coming back from the dead. Close-up, this is a tough concept to comprehend. A favorite author mine, Barbara Brown Taylor says this: "The resurrection is the one and only event in Jesus' life that was entirely between him and God. There were no witnesses whatsoever. No one on earth can say what happened inside that tomb, because no one was there. All the witnesses arrived after the fact. Two of them saw clothes. One saw an angel. Most saw nothing at all because they were still in

---

[3] http://www.radiolab.org/story/goo-and-you/Jan 28, 2014

bed that morning, but it turned out that did not matter because the empty tomb was not the point."[4]

The resurrection is at the core of Christianity. Some people ask: "Am I supposed to simply believe this teaching when it's impossible to understand?" I appreciate that people want to know how the resurrection worked. Curiosity and questions are good. Yet, the primary truth is built on an event that cannot be explained. No one got to see how death was transformed into life inside a dark tomb. For many people this becomes an obstacle to faith in God and the Christian Church.

However, every day we believe in or put our trust in things we don't first try to figure out and understand. We get into planes, trusting aerodynamics that most of us could no more explain than we could flap our arms and fly to Finland.

Every morning we get up with the expectation that today will not be the day on which gravity will expire, leaving us all to float off into airless space like astronauts in orbit.

Every day we offer ourselves to science without giving it much thought. Some of us are dependent on a drug or a medical device to continue life or the next heartbeat. But it is a rare person that would reject a pacemaker because they cannot explain how it works.

---

[4] Barbara Brown Taylor www.religion-online.org/showarticle.asp?title=640

I'm grateful there are intelligent people with the gift for the scientific. I am content to believe their assertions about aerodynamics, gravity and all things scientific, even though I cannot understand, nor do I seek to have it all explained before I trust.

Isn't it odd that while we take the miracles of modern science, engineering and electronics on faith, some people want facts in order to have faith in God?

We are less logical and rational than we like to think. We trust the experts of science and medicine with our lives, even in the absence of complete understanding. So, it is not really a question of having faith. We all put faith in a variety of things. The quest is to what, or to whom, shall we entrust the dimension of faith in the divine, in God, and ultimately in the resurrection of Jesus from the dead?

So, using two brief science lessons I want to look at this biblical account of resurrection. We start with a grieving woman named Mary. She is trudging in the dark to a tomb on that first Easter morning, only to be shocked to find the risen Jesus there.

First lesson: In science there is what is called the theory of the black box. It's used to define things in terms of input and output, without any knowledge of the in-between in what is called the black box.

In this story of Easter, the input is the man Jesus (a teacher, healer, miracle-worker--a guy of some incredible claims). The output is Jesus back from the dead, the risen

Christ, just as he said he would be. Yet in the tomb we have no idea how this amazing transformation occurred--the theory of the black box.

That brings me to the second science lesson. Recently I listened to a podcast "Goo and You" on Radiolab, a show which seeks to illuminate ideas where boundaries blur between science, philosophy, and human experience."

This podcast explored the mystery of the metamorphosis that occurs when a caterpillar becomes a butterfly inside the chrysalis. It's one of the least understood and most complicated black boxes in nature. *Input:* caterpillar. But inside that most mysterious black box, hormones pump and genetics turn on. The caterpillar, before it becomes a butterfly softens into an undifferentiated, goo-like substance inside that black box.

At this point everything is changing. The output, what emerges and takes flight is completely different from the input and yet it is continuous with the creature that crawled in.

Black boxes, empty tombs, and goo. Easter means change, transformation, new life, and faith in something we cannot explain. Mary, the disciples and billions of people over the centuries have been transformed to have faith in something hopeful because of the resurrection of Jesus.

After all the years I have been in this endeavor of believing, I cannot explain how faith transforms, but I can see that it does. I have seen it happen in many of you over the years. I hear it in the experiences people tell me when in major life-wrenching changes-- when they have every good reason to despair and be disbelieving in God, instead, because of faith in Jesus, they find hope, even peace and joy.

The Good News this day, my friends, is true. Death is conquered and life triumphs--because God raised Jesus from the dead. We cannot explain it-- the tomb remains a black box. But what has come forth and what continues to change lives is the output of God's amazing, mysterious love for you and all creation. Christ is risen. Alleluia. Amen!

Please Pass the Salt

Matthew 5: 13-20

Jesus said: 'You are the salt of the earth; but if salt has lost its taste, how can its saltiness be restored? It is no longer good for anything but is thrown out and trampled underfoot.

'You are the light of the world. A city built on a hill cannot be hidden. No one after lighting a lamp puts it under the bushel basket, but on the lampstand, and it gives light to all in the house. In the same way, let your light shine before others, so that they may see your good works and give glory to your Father in heaven.

'Do not think that I have come to abolish the law or the prophets; I have come not to abolish but to fulfil. For truly I tell you, until heaven and earth pass away, not one letter, not one stroke of a letter, will pass from the law until all is accomplished. Therefore, whoever breaks one of the least of these commandments, and teaches others to do the same, will be called least in the kingdom of heaven; but whoever does them and teaches them will be called great in the kingdom of heaven. For I tell you, unless your righteousness exceeds that of the scribes and Pharisees, you will never enter the kingdom of heaven.

Dear Sisters and Brothers in Christ, may grace and peace be with you.

I grew up in a traditional family where it was common for my parents and three siblings to sit down at the kitchen table for supper each evening. My memory does not have us missing too many evenings together. In those days, this was common, and the myriad of reasons families do not do this anymore did not exist back then.

My mom did not work outside the home and my dad came home from work about 5:30 every evening. As soon as my dad arrived home, my mom began putting the meal on the table. Over the years, our meal time practices stayed intact. We prayed together. We practiced our manners. We tried whatever new food mom had provided, but not always cheerfully. We talked about the day's events. Those things all passed the test of time.

One thing that did change over those years was the place of the salt shaker on the table. Somewhere during my growing up years, picking up the shaker to add salt to food became a grain of controversy.

I am not sure when the salt shaker became a container of controversy at our table. Perhaps it was when the AMA published a study linking salt in the diet to increased rates of hypertension. I know my mom's brother who was a pharmacist waged his own war on salt. He was known to say to a person he saw using the salt shaker "If you want to shake away your life, keep salting."

I think it was about then that the salt shaker disappeared from our table and it was no longer safe to say, "Please pass the salt."

This Bible reading counters any practice of banning salt. In it we, as followers of Jesus, are called "salt of the earth." This reading follows the Beatitudes and is part of a series of teachings called the "Sermon on the Mount."

In Jesus' teaching of the Beatitudes he announces that the kingdom of God has come for all, no matter if you are hungry or well-fed, poor or rich, happy or sad. The kingdom of God is an inclusive reality, a promise without boundaries.

Now Jesus tells how we have a part in bringing this kingdom of God to others. He says, *"You are the salt of the earth. You are light for the world."*

So, pick up the shaker and shake away. Beam your light for all to see, and by shaking and beaming you'll show the world this kingdom of God.

The truth is salt is only effective when it's applied. Salt left to itself is just salt. It does not do anything. Salt needs to interact with something in order to be useful. Salt on the highway surface or your tongue makes a difference, right? You are salt of the earth for shaking grains of grace and thereby extending to others the kingdom of God. How have you been salt lately? Where have you been shaking grains of God's good kingdom to make a difference at work, school, home, and beyond?

"You are the light of the world," Jesus says. Who is seeing the light of God's love through you?

In recent days, amid protests across the country and great debate in the public arena on a variety of highly-charged topics, how have you been salt and light for the kingdom of God? How has God used you to bring some better flavor and some reassuring light into this world?

It seems that, if ever there was a time when we in this world needed salt and light, it's right now. Check the headlines; listen to the news; glance over the social media pages. There is an unusually pervasive sense of dis-ease in our world and division in our country.

Every day you have the privilege of depositing grains of grace and shining rays of light to bring the mercy, welcome and grace of God's kingdom to the world.

So where will you go after you leave worship to spread some salt and beam some light? The best direction I find comes from Jesus' words we heard last week. When Jesus called a huge crowd of people 'blessed' there were disagreements and divisions between them. But Jesus called them all blessed. He said God's kingdom had come for all of them.

Today, disagreements and divisions between people in this country seem to have increased significantly. We disagree on many things. We disagree about what's right and what's wrong. We disagree about what's good and what's evil. We disagree about who's safe and who is to be feared. We disagree about who should receive our welcome and who should not.

This is a difficult time for many people and for many reasons. We need salt and light in this world. And the crazy thing is that God has already provided it...right in and through you and us, a congregation of salty and shining people with a mission to bring forth the kingdom of God.

May you be inspired, even as you are blessed, to bring the kingdom to all within your reach, shaking grains of grace and beaming rays of hope. Amen.

Showdown in the Desert

Matthew 4:1-11

Then Jesus was led up by the Spirit into the wilderness to be tempted by the devil. He fasted for forty days and forty nights, and afterwards he was famished. The tempter came and said to him, 'If you are the Son of God, command these stones to become loaves of bread.' But he answered, 'It is written,

"One does not live by bread alone, but by every word that comes from the mouth of God."'

Then the devil took him to the holy city and placed him on the pinnacle of the temple, saying to him, 'If you are the Son of God, throw yourself down; for it is written,

"He will command his angels concerning you" and "On their hands they will bear you up, so that you will not dash your foot against a stone."'

Jesus said to him, 'Again it is written, "Do not put the Lord your God to the test."'

Again, the devil took him to a very high mountain and showed him all the kingdoms of the world and their splendor; and he said to him, 'All these I will give you, if you will fall down and worship me.' Jesus said to him, 'Away with you, Satan! for it is written, "Worship the Lord your God, and serve only him"'

Then the devil left him, and suddenly angels came and waited on him.

Dear Friends:

Every so often I have this recurring dream. I dream that I'm back visiting the campus of Luther Seminary where I received a degree many years ago. In my dream the time is the present day. As I'm strolling the campus I bump into the Registrar, Carol Baker. She is quick to greet me and smile, but soon is reminding me that I have yet to finish some class work. It seems that way back then, years ago, I never finished a test in Dr. Sponheim's class. After all this time Carol is still expecting me to complete the class. She reminds me that the Incomplete will turn to a failing grade if I don't finish the work soon. It's an awful dream and I usually wake up tense after Ms. Baker walks away.

The dream may say a lot about me, but it also reminds me of how much I disliked tests. From Mrs. Kleve's spelling tests in 7th grade to Mr. Rubin's drop quizzes in 12th grade Psychology class, I've never liked tests. To this day, I wonder if tests really accomplished that much. Yes, they forced me to study, but I wonder if they instilled any fruitful learning.

I have learned that tests didn't end when I got my Master's degree. Life is filled with tests.

- Teenagers tests parents' patience.

- Spouses test each other's commitment to marriage.

- Cancer diagnoses test our faith.

- Aging tests our tenacity.

- Employees test our generosity.

- Students test our abilities to effectively teach.

We just can't seem to get away from tests, no matter our age or station in life.

Well, in the Bible reading from Matthew, Satan is giving Jesus a test. This scene is a get-acquainted session between Jesus and Satan. Why Satan thinks he is in charge, so he gets to give the test, we're not told.

There are some things that I notice quickly in this scene. First, only Jesus and Satan are present. Second, there are three tests Satan gives Jesus:

1. Turn stone into bread

2. "Worship me" Satan says, and "I'll give you the whole world (as if it were Satan's to give).

3. Jump from a high place, in order to prove God's promise of physical safety.

The third thing I notice in this scene is that Jesus never finishes any of the tests Satan presents. He gets an "Incomplete" grade. All Jesus does is quote Scripture and leaves it at that.

Now, I don't know about you, but I wonder: Why was Jesus reluctant to jump in and ace these tests? Surely, He could have passed all three tests. But he does not even try. That troubles me.

Later, on Good Friday to be exact, Jesus is nailed to a cross and we hear Satan test Jesus again. This time it's a criminal who says to Jesus, "Aren't you the Christ? Save yourself and us." The people in the crowd watching Jesus die chime in: "Yeah Jesus, come down from the cross, and we'll believe in you ...get your God to rescue you." But again, Jesus doesn't ace the test.

Are you troubled that Jesus doesn't stand up for himself? Any teacher today would give Jesus an F for failing to try, much less, live up to his potential. All this makes me wonder about Jesus and subsequently about God. By looking at this scene in the wilderness between Jesus and Satan, I see a seemingly weak God.

If I would have been Jesus' coach, his personal trainer in the wilderness that day I would have pushed him to do his best. I would have had him running drills: "Okay Jesus, here's the stone. That's what bread looks like. Now, change it, pronto. And let's do it again. Oh, and Jesus, don't be afraid of heights, you can jump, take a deep breath, close your eyes, and whatever you do, bend your knees and you'll land just fine. We'll show Satan he doesn't hold a candle to your abilities Jesus. You can do it!"

Alright, I ask you, wouldn't you rather have a more proactive, take-charge kind of God? Would you have advised Jesus to deflect all of Satan's tests? "Just quote Scripture Jesus, that'll do it. Yeah, that'll put Satan in his place."

I don't think so. I think most people would rather see a God who knows how to stand up to the test, to put the pedal to the metal and wow that little punk Satan with cosmic powers.

Well, we know the outcome of story of Jesus and Satan in the wilderness. This story reveals a profound difference between God's power and Satan's power.

Satan is one who can dazzle, coerce, use force and destroy. Surely, we human beings have learned much from that kind of power. Governments use that kind of dazzling, coercive power all the time. With a billy club or an AK-47 or a F-15 fighter plane, human beings can force other human beings to do just about anything they want. This kind of power, like Satan's power is coercive; it forces, and it threatens.

In contrast, God's power is just the opposite. God's power is noncoercive, it doesn't force. God's power commits to transform humans gently, from the inside out. On the face, this kind of power may seem at times like weakness.

Satan's power is a take-charge, forceful means to achieve the goal. God's power is totally different. I'll admit that there are times I wish God's power came across as more decisive.

Just think about it. If God would adopt a decisive, fast acting role in world affairs, life would be different for so many people. Imagine if God had merely reached down and flicked Saddam Hussein off the throne 15 years ago, how many lives would have been saved in the warring madness of the Middle East? If God had done that, think of the billions of dollars that, instead of going to military might could have been spent to educate children and provide safe water, food, housing to improve the global standard of living for billions of people! Imagine today's world without 60 million refugees, if only God had tied the hands of Syrian president Bashar al-Assad.

If God were more decisive and quick-acting in the world, God could have stomped out Hitler and vicious hate. Millions of Jews could have been spared.

From a global to a personal level: doesn't it seem at times like God is just sitting on God's hands? How nice would it be to have quick and clear answers to prayer? I would take up much less of God's time if God answered my prayers more quickly. I would like God to be more active in healing diseases, providing protection and safety for the innocent and vulnerable. I would like God to seem less ambiguous for the sake of my doubting friends.

When I think these thoughts, I recognize in myself a thin, hollow echo of the challenge that Satan hurled at Jesus that day in the wilderness. God resists those temptations now as Jesus resisted them on earth, settling instead for a slower, gentler, wiser way.

The more I look at Jesus here in the wilderness with Satan, the more I am impressed with his miracle of restraint. More amazing is Jesus' refusal to perform and to overwhelm Satan in the face of his temptations. I believe God insists on such restraint because God knows no big powerful displays will achieve the desired response.

What is the response God desires from us? Power? No. Decisiveness? Not really. Love? Yes. Jesus does not want our obedience to come from our fear of God's power or force. Rather, in restraint demonstrated by Jesus, God wants us to act out of faithfulness and love.

You know, never in the Bible do we see Jesus doing any arm-twisting. Jesus did not demand with force, any kind of behavior from another person. Jesus didn't play any games.

There is the encounter between Jesus and a rich young man who asks Jesus: "What must I do to inherit eternal life?" Jesus, the Bible says, looked at the young man and loved him and then answered with uncompromising words "Go and sell what you have and give the money to the poor and then come and follow me." The young man could not bring himself to do it and he walked away, and Jesus let him leave. There was not any verbal bashing, bullying, no arm-twisting; no mind games. Jesus showed restraint and did not force the young man.

Even in the final scenes of Jesus' life before he was killed, Jesus knew that Judas was going to betray him. But Jesus did not try to prevent that evil deed. Again, Jesus' restraint came shining through.

Like that day in the wilderness, Jesus and Satan did battle--a very quiet, subtly powerful battle. Do you wonder who won? Though Jesus rebuffed Satan three times, Satan may well have departed from the confrontation wearing a smirk. "Yeah sure, this Jesus guy has power. Seems like a chicken to me."

But at the end of the story, when practically everyone on earth thought that Jesus had thrown in the towel, accepted the failing grade, God's power came blasting through an empty grave.

My friends, when you feel the temptations rising in your life, remember Jesus. And rejoice, that our God has a power in restraint, made known in love.

The Unmeasured Neighbor

Luke 10: 25-37

Just then a lawyer stood up to test Jesus. 'Teacher,' he said, 'what must I do to inherit eternal life?' He said to him, 'What is written in the law? What do you read there?' He answered, 'You shall love the Lord your God with all your heart, and with all your soul, and with all your strength, and with all your mind; and your neighbor as yourself.' And he said to him, 'You have given the right answer; do this, and you will live.'

But wanting to justify himself, he asked Jesus, 'And who is my neighbor?' Jesus replied, 'A man was going down from Jerusalem to Jericho, and fell into the hands of robbers, who stripped him, beat him, and went away, leaving him half dead. Now by chance a priest was going down that road; and when he saw him, he passed by on the other side. So likewise a Levite, when he came to the place and saw him, passed by on the other side. But a Samaritan while travelling came near him; and when he saw him, he was moved with pity. He went to him and bandaged his wounds, having poured oil and wine on them. Then he put him on his own animal, brought him to an inn, and took care of him. The next day he took out two denarii, gave them to the innkeeper, and said, "Take care of him; and when I come back, I will repay you whatever more you spend." Which of these three, do you think, was a neighbor to the man who fell into the hands of the robbers?' He said, 'The one who showed him mercy.' Jesus said to him, 'Go and do likewise.'

Note: This was the final sermon preached by Pastor Kurt Jacobson at Trinity Lutheran Church, Eau Claire, WI on July 16, 2016.

Dear Sisters and Brothers, may the grace and peace we inherit from the generous spirit of God be yours in abundance, today and always.

This morning we come to one of the most familiar stories of the Bible and it just happens to be the final one I'll share with you. It has always been an honor to be in this very spot to dig into God's Word with you. It's been a pleasure to see how God's Word has prospered your lives. I've watched it encourage, inform, redirect and provide you hope. As a congregation I've seen how God's Word has moved us forward and outward to extend the grace and mercy of Jesus to people in need. This Word has transformed how we think--opening us to encompass a wider circle of humanity and counter the divisive tendencies of society and human nature.

When we built a mission statement together in 2000, God's Word infused the minds of the 100 people who were directly involved in crafting it: *"Serving in Christ's Love and Sharing the Good News."* The Word and this mission have enlivened and empowered us to serve others, blessing thousands of people with food and shelter, offering healing, literally saving people from despair.

In short, the Word of God has been a wellspring of life for this church and its mission. Today, as I say goodbye, the

Word from Jesus as Luke tells it, reminds us that the mission continues, it never ends. For the joy of being part of all this with you-- thank you.

So, let's get to the Word today. This story often called the Good Samaritan is known widely--even to people who have little familiarity with the Bible. Some believe this Good Samaritan story is the basis for public law, which forces us to render care to someone in need or protects us from liability should we help someone and in turn be sued.

It all started in an encounter between Jesus and a lawyer, an educated man of Jewish tradition, who asks: "What must I do to inherit eternal life?" Now, there is irony here. A person does not do anything to inherit. An inheritance is a gift from the giver.

Jesus knows this guy is smart. In Jewish tradition the lawyer would already know the answer, which has been taught him since childhood. So, Jesus asks, "What do you read in the Law" (meaning, in the Old Testament books which Jews would know by heart).

The lawyer: "Love the Lord your God and love your neighbor as yourself."

Jesus: "Do this and you will live."

But the lawyer can't leave good enough alone. So, he asks, "Who is my neighbor?"

Right here I like to imagine the mental conversation this guy was having with himself. I imagine he might have been really wanting to ask: *How far do I have to take this loving thing, Jesus?* Or more importantly, *Who can I leave outside the boundaries of my love and care? I am not everyone's keeper, am I? There must be limits, right?*

But Jesus is not going to let this guy off easy. I think Jesus wanted to say "Not so fast wise guy. You want a definition of neighbor? Pay attention, then."

Jesus tells the story. There was a man who was traveling on a road. Beset by thieves and beaten within an inch of his life, this unnamed traveler can only survive if a stranger will help him. Jesus recounts that both a priest and a Levite (good people of Jewish tradition like the lawyer himself) pass by without assisting this victim. However, Jesus does not explain why they do not stop to help. We can try to guess why. Maybe they feared blood. Maybe they were late for a kid's soccer game or some important meeting. Maybe they were just tired after a long day of work and they wanted to get home, into comfortable clothes and some time with no one asking anything of them. Perhaps this priest and Levite are not so much villains, as normal people with whom we can identify.

How many of us have not gone through the same moral calculus when passing a person in need, whether a homeless person on the sidewalk or a driver sitting by a car with a flat tire? Alas, accounts of people finding reasons not to come to someone's aid are just as common as people in need. But, in the end, Jesus does not tell us why a priest and Levite do not help. All we know is that someone else was willing.

As Jesus continues the story, a third person comes upon this beaten up guy. We are told he is a Samaritan. He springs into action. He goes to extraordinary lengths of effort and time as well as personal expense and he saves the man's life. He is a stellar example of compassion, generosity and selflessness.

The rub in Jesus' story--in his answer to the lawyer's question about who is his neighbor--comes in the pedigree of this caregiver. Samaritans were despised by mainstream Jews. They were considered foreigners, even enemies. Jesus shatters this lawyer's thinking, his mindset, his attitudes and his biases by having a Samaritan be the one who renders care.

We usually hear this story as an exhortation to do good, to help the stranger in need. This is true and necessary, especially in a world so often characterized by our neglect of one another. Our ability to ignore the plight of others is breathtaking, and often backed up by our unwillingness to see every human being as a brother or sister.

But I think there's something more personally provoking and profound that Jesus is getting at in telling this story. It's a message critical to us individually, as a congregation, and the human family.

Perhaps you remember the Seinfeld show. In its final episode NBC has accepted Jerry's proposal for a show. The network offers Jerry the company jet to take him anywhere he desires. Soon after Jerry, Elaine, George and Kramer are winging their way to Paris. However, not long after taking off the plane must make an emergency landing due to Kramer's water-logged ear. As this comic quarter waits a few hours in a small town, they see an obese man being car-jacked. True to form, they make fun of the man, but are soon arrested under a new Good Samaritan law for failing to help. While sitting in jail waiting for a court hearing, the foursome tries to grasp why they were arrested. They wonder aloud why there would be a law requiring their involvement in a situation for which they have no responsibility? In their view that's what nuns and the Red Cross are for, not ordinary people like themselves.

Throughout its nine years on TV, Seinfeld's characters used, ridiculed, and made fun of everyone they met. The show often humorously pointed out our foibles and follies, but the characters were always self-centered, and we laughed, because we could see ourselves in them.

The lawyer asked Jesus "Who is my neighbor?" hoping he could remain self-centered and justify not extending mercy to someone in need.

In telling this story of a foreigner rendering care, Jesus in effect says to the lawyer, "Look, you're asking the wrong question?" The real question is not "Who is my neighbor? It doesn't make any difference who your neighbor is out there because, if you say you love God, then you should extend mercy to all."

What Jesus is getting at in this story, which is provocative and profound, is not simply the question "Who is my neighbor?" but rather "Am I a neighbor?"

It is a question of mission--of getting outside of ourselves--of letting go of our biases and judgements-- and getting into the mode of mercy which flows right from the heart of God.

A person who has been given the love of God (and you have) will respond with compassion to human suffering no matter who, what or why. The Samaritan shows us the heart of God.

Mercy for another human being cannot be qualified by race, nationality, religion, gender, orientation or any other barrier that we might erect. This lawyer was looking for where he could stop loving. Jesus said: It is precisely in sharing love and being merciful that one becomes a neighbor.

By the end of this scene, the lawyer has it right. Jesus asks: "Which of these three guys, the priest, Levite or the Samaritan was the neighbor to the man in need."

Lawyer: "The one who showed him mercy."
Jesus: "Go and do likewise."

My friends, may the love of God that is yours in abundance direct your mercy, mark your neighborliness and always enliven your mission together as the people of Trinity Lutheran Church. Amen.

Waiting on God

Luke 2:22-38

When the time came for their purification according to the law of Moses, they brought him up to Jerusalem to present him to the Lord (as it is written in the law of the Lord, 'Every firstborn male shall be designated as holy to the Lord'), and they offered a sacrifice according to what is stated in the law of the Lord, 'a pair of turtle-doves or two young pigeons.'

Now there was a man in Jerusalem whose name was Simeon; this man was righteous and devout, looking forward to the consolation of Israel, and the Holy Spirit rested on him. It had been revealed to him by the Holy Spirit that he would not see death before he had seen the Lord's Messiah. Guided by the Spirit, Simeon came into the temple; and when the parents brought in the child Jesus, to do for him what was customary under the law, Simeon took him in his arms and praised God, saying,

'Master, now you are dismissing your servant in peace, according to your word;

for my eyes have seen your salvation, which you have prepared in the presence of all peoples,

a light for revelation to the Gentiles and for glory to your people Israel.'

And the child's father and mother were amazed at what was being said about him. Then Simeon blessed them and said to his mother Mary, 'This child is destined for the falling and the rising of many in Israel, and to be a sign that will be opposed so that the inner thoughts of many will be revealed—and a sword will pierce your own soul too.'

There was also a prophet, Anna the daughter of Phanuel, of the tribe of Asher. She was of a great age, having lived with her husband for seven years after her marriage, then as a widow to the age of eighty-four. She never left the temple but worshipped there with fasting and prayer night and day. At that moment she came and began to praise God and to speak about the child to all who were looking for the redemption of Jerusalem.

Dear Friends, on this seventh day of Christmas, grace and peace to you.

Christmas has passed once again and while we are done waiting for the celebration, we still wait. We wait for the fulfillment of Jesus' promise to come again and make all things new.

The Bible reading you just heard introduces us to a couple of people who spent their lives waiting for God. Simeon and Anna--faithful people who show us that waiting is part of the life of faith. This truth presents us with an immediate challenge.

Think of it. We are not born with the ability to wait. Babies are not born with a capacity to be patient. Children must be taught how to wait. Parents must possess enormous patience to accomplish this teaching. The ability to wait comes with maturity, but it is something we must work to develop. Waiting is a discipline to be learned. In the context of belief and faith in God, waiting for God becomes a spiritual discipline.

This world we inhabit does not help make us better at waiting. The mode of American society is for faster everything! I bought the newest iPad this fall, and it still seems a bit slow to me. I still have to wait for documents to download and apps to open. There are so many things which can be hard to wait for. It's hard:

- waiting for celebrations with family or friends;

- waiting for the plane carrying the one we love;

- waiting for the morning to relieve the sleepless night;

- waiting for one's suffering to cease;

- waiting for the new pastor to be named and the interim period to end.

It is never easy to wait.

A woman was waiting in the checkout line at a department store shortly before Christmas. As she waited she was fuming. In her cart was a broom, along with some cleaning supplies. For those in the line nearby, she made it clear she was not happy to be waiting to check out. When she finally reached the cashier, the barcode on the broom didn't scan. The cashier called for a price check which added to the wait, prompting the woman to remark indignantly: "Well, I'll be lucky to get out of here and home before Christmas!" Picking up on her comment, the clerk replied to the woman: "Don't worry, ma'am. With the wind kicking up out there, and that new broom you'll be home in no time."

I am not very good at waiting. Are you? I have yet to master the spiritual discipline of waiting. I need all the help I can get when it comes on waiting for God.

Simeon and Anna had been waiting for the Messiah who had been foretold for generations. The Bible tells us Simeon was a priest and Anna was an eighty-four-year-old widow who never left the temple, but worshiped day and night. They were waiting for God's promise of a savior to be fulfilled. From them, we have clues on how to develop the spiritual discipline of waiting.

Have you ever waited for God? Have you waited for answer to prayer? Have you ever waited for God to heal your body, mind or heart; relieve you of worry or grief? Have you ever waited for God to guide you and show you a path for your life?

I have had times of waiting for God and in the more intense waits, I wish I had thought of Simeon and Anna. From them I learn that to develop the spiritual discipline of waiting--one cannot be passive. They were active while waiting. "Night and day" Anna was actively waiting, "serving God" the bible tells us.

To develop the ability to wait one must be active, not passive. While we often believe to wait means to sit and do nothing, waiting for God is more like waiting for an honored guest to arrive at your home. There is much to be done preparing to receive the one who is to come.

Developing the spiritual discipline of waiting requires being active. Today's Bible reading helps us on this front. Active waiting involves doing the things Jesus calls us to do: pray unceasingly, tend to the creation, serve those in need, forgive everyone, care for all God's creatures, share what you have. Simeon and Anna did such things while they waited for God to reveal the promised savior.

Not long before his death, Henri Nouwen, a Catholic priest and noted author wrote a book called *Sabbatical Journey*[5]. In it he wrote about his trapeze artists friends, the Flying Roudellas. The Roudellas explained that there is a special relationship between the flyer and the catcher. This relationship is governed by important rules, such as the flyer is the one who let's go, and the catcher is the one who catches.

As the flyer swings on the trapeze high above the crowd, the moment comes when she must let go. As she does, she flings her body out in mid-air. At that point, her

---

[5] Nouwen, Henri "Sabbatical Journey," Crossroads Publishing Co, 1998

sole task is to wait for the strong hands of the catcher to take hold of her at the right moment.

One of the Flying Roudellas told Nouwen, "The flyer must never try to catch the catcher. The flyer's job is to fly, while waiting in absolute trust. The catcher will catch her, but she must wait."

When we wait for God, for whatever reason, to help, heal or direct, it is possible to get ahead of God. We wait, and nothing seems to happen, so we get impatient and start trying to work things out on our own. In short, we start trying to catch God instead of waiting for God to catch us. Waiting is a period of learning, not a static state. Waiting is a time when God is working on us, behind the scenes, often unknown.

Simeon and Anna waited actively for God with absolute trust. They worked and worshiped, performed acts of justice and prayer. They did what they could, and they waited faithfully.

I fully expect that for the rest of my life, there will be times when any kind of waiting will be a challenge. But when it comes to waiting for God, I hope to do better. Here Simeon informs me again. When he saw baby Jesus in the temple that day he was filled with joy. His wait for God was over. He said: *"My eyes have seen the salvation of God."* Simeon's wait for God ended with the ultimate gift.

My friends, while we wait, may we be active in extending to others and this world, the fruits of faithfulness, inspired by the promise that at the end of our waiting, God will come and fulfill us with the ultimate gift, too.

Where Everyone Has a Place of Honor

Luk 14:1, 7-14

On one occasion when Jesus was going to the house of a leader of the Pharisees to eat a meal on the sabbath, they were watching him closely.

When he noticed how the guests chose the places of honor, he told them a parable. 'When you are invited by someone to a wedding banquet, do not sit down at the place of honor, in case someone more distinguished than you has been invited by your host; and the host who invited both of you may come and say to you, "Give this person your place", and then in disgrace you would start to take the lowest place. But when you are invited, go and sit down at the lowest place, so that when your host comes, he may say to you, "Friend, move up higher"; then you will be honored in the presence of all who sit at the table with you. For all who exalt themselves will be humbled, and those who humble themselves will be exalted.'

He said also to the one who had invited him, 'When you give a luncheon or a dinner, do not invite your friends or your brothers or your relatives or rich neighbors, in case they may invite you in return, and you would be repaid. But when you give a banquet, invite the poor, the crippled, the lame, and the blind. And you will be blessed, because they cannot repay you, for you will be repaid at the resurrection of the righteous.'

Dear Sisters and Brothers in Christ, grace and peace be with you all.

This story of Jesus at a dinner party makes me think of a game that we all learn to play in our lives. It's the game that does not really have a name, but we all know it. The goal of the game is to be important and the success provides players a feeling that you belong, that you matter. Kids learn to play this game early in life on sports fields (where much of their lives take place now) and in the school cafeteria. Learning there occurs when the kid you thought was your good friend turns his back on you to sit with the "cool kids" --leaving you to know clearly that you are not one of them. You are not included. You do not belong. Playing the game does not always lead to happy endings.

For those of us far along in the span of life, we still keep an eye on this game, but hopefully we do not play it as often as we did in those years when we were striving to build ourselves in careers, in social circles and the like.

Some years ago, I met a young man who had finished law school and was learning to play the game on the field of what he hoped was his budding career. In the endeavor of interviewing for positions at law firms that he viewed as prestigious, he deduced that one of the ways of playing the game applied to what he ordered for dinner while at an interview. After a couple of interviews, he noticed that there seemed to be a culture of food expressed on these occasions … all the firm's personnel involved in the interview ordered similar entrees. So, this young man decided it would be wise to order a similar menu item to send a signal that he was able to blend in with the culture of the firm, even to the food he ate.

At one interview, the lawyers from the firm were ordering big slabs of red meat. So, this young man ordered prime rib with a horseradish glaze. Waiting for the food, the interview began, and this young man realized there was a culture of toughness, manliness, machismo about the interviewing team. So, he decided he would play the game and do his best to appear manly and tough.

The food came. The candidate cut a big piece of prime rib, dripping with horseradish. He put it in his mouth at the moment one of the lawyers asked, "So, Dave, tell us why you are looking at a firm so far from your hometown." And at that moment, tears sprang into his eyes, because he had a mouthful of horseradish. He spent the next several minutes trying to wipe away what was now a stream of tears, choking down the food in his mouth, hoping to convince this table of tough guys that he was not crying at the thought of leaving home. He did not get an offer from that firm.

The Bible reading before us today has a lot of game playing going on. Here we find Jesus unwilling to join in playing.

Here is the setting. Jesus is invited to a prestigious dinner party. It ranks as a high-level social invitation

because it's thrown by a "leader of the Pharisees."
Pharisees were the elite of the Jewish religious
establishment. Prior to this dinner party, the Pharisees have
criticized Jesus for breaking several religious rules and
associating with sinners and working on the Sabbath. Jesus'
has been invited not because he is considered an equal, but
because he is a curiosity who has been garnering lots of
attention around town.

While at the party, Jesus watches people jockeying for
position, playing the game, and the goal is to get the places
of greatest honor around the dinner table.

A little time out here to envision the table around which
the guests of the Pharisee are sitting. In Jesus' day, tables at
a dinner party were low to the floor and guests would
recline on low couches around the table. The table would
form a U and the host would sit at the bottom of the U. The
guests that ranked with greatest honor would be the seats
immediately to the host's right and left. From there out to
each end of the U would be declining places of honor until
the outermost seats at the ends of the legs of the U. Those
people washed the dishes at the end of the evening. Just
kidding.

Now you have the setting of this scene where the guests
are playing the game hoping to get as close as possible to
the host and the seats of honor. Apparently, it was common
for guests who were not sure of their status, to arrive early,
and try to judge where it would be safe to sit. This was
done in order to avoid the humiliation of being asked to

give up the seat for a more important person. On the other hand, the important people could arrive fashionably late, make a grand entrance, and be confident that their host would boot anyone who had been so foolish as to take the seat that was rightfully theirs.

Now, this was a brutal game. The potential insults inherent in this game did not end with the seating order. The guests who landed the lesser seats also received lesser quality food. While the honored guests would get the elegant dishes, the choicest morsels, the rest of the table got food that reminds me of a line from the Woody Allen movie *"Annie Hall."* "There's an old joke, um... two elderly women are at a Catskill mountain resort, and one of 'em says, "Boy, the food at this place is really terrible." The other one says, "Yeah, I know; and such small portions."

As dinner begins, are you wondering like I am, what prompted Jesus to accept the invitation in the first place. I would rather be having a root canal than dining with these guys who are so critical and judgmental.

As the guests begin to sit at the table, Jesus decides it's time for more than small talk. What ensues is a lesson in how to lose friends and alienate people. But maybe more so, a lesson on the futility of playing the game of who is popular and most important.

So, Jesus offers a critique using a few verses from Proverbs. It always helps to remember that Jesus is a Jew, steeped in scripture, and he offers this Proverb to point out the folly of the guests clamoring for the honored seats. *Do not put yourself forward in the king's presence or stand in the place of the great; for it is better to be told, "Come up here," than to be put lower in the presence of a noble. ~ Proverbs 25:6-7*

Humiliation is to be put lower in the presence of a noble; to be seated at a table in the cafeteria all by yourself while the cool kids laugh together at another table nearby; to feel that you've made an utter fool of yourself in front of the people you were hoping might hire you.

Jesus watches as people set themselves up for the risk of humiliation in a quest to feel they are important, that they matter. And you know, I think his heart goes out to them, he has compassion for them. He says this: *The way to get honor is to humble yourself. The way to be invited into the better seat is to take the worse seat.*

Next, Jesus goes a step further and addresses the host. Jesus wants to see an end to the game entirely and as he turns to the host, Jesus does two things. First, Jesus gently reproaches the host for offering the playing field for the game in the first place. *'When you give a luncheon or a dinner, do not invite your friends or your brothers or your relatives or rich neighbors, in case they may invite you in return, and you would be repaid.* After all, the Pharisee is the one who has invited people of varying social ranks to a feast, he is the one whose guests are, apparently, a little bit panicked about where they will sit. He is the one who, by inviting all those guests, will undoubtedly receive return invitations and, given his position as leader of the Pharisees, he will surely be in the place of honor at all those feasts. Jesus calls him on this: the hidden agenda of the host, the desire to be the center of attention at his own dinners and at the others to which he is invited. Jesus calls upon the host to stop the game altogether.

The second thing Jesus does is to offer a truly radical alternative. *But when you give a banquet, invite the poor, the crippled, the lame, and the blind. And you will be blessed, because they cannot repay you, for you will be repaid at the resurrection of the righteous.'*

Jesus says, forget your usual guest list. Forget the "you scratch my back, I'll scratch yours" usual way of doing things. Do something entirely different. Invite those of no social rank whatsoever, those entirely without the means to return the honor with an invitation of their own. Jesus urges the Pharisee to invite the poor, the crippled, the blind and the lame, those whom no one invites.

It's hard to overstate just how shocking this suggestion is. Back then the poor, crippled people had no status. They were considered impure and the Pharisees are hyper-vigilant about laws of purity. So, Jesus is compelling this dinner host to invite precisely those people whom he probably spends his days avoiding.

Jesus is taking a hard look at society's notions of who's in and who's out, who's up and who's down, and he is turning it all on its head.

My friends, for us today, for all people right now, Jesus is offering us a vision of a fresh start, a new world, one that has nothing to do with playing the game. Jesus is offering us a vision of the kingdom of God. It's a vision of a feast table at which no one has a place of honor, because everyone is in the place of honor. Everyone is welcome. All people equally honored guests, because it is God who extends the invitation.

Good news? Good news for you? I hope so. I see good news for any who have ever felt like they don't have the same status as others and have been humiliated or eliminated from being included in places like the lunchroom, the soccer field or … the church.

There is challenge in this good news for us and for Christian churches all over the world: to express and enact in our attitudes and actions this vision of the kingdom of God where all are welcome, where no one is more important than another, where no one is excluded on any basis, where nothing of our position or rank in society necessitates playing the game to earn a sense of inclusion or belonging.

I am hopeful about this congregation's ability to extend this vision of the kingdom of God to so many people who are looking for, and have yet to find in Christian churches, the goodness of a genuine journey of faith together, where no one plays games, where the table is open, and every seat at the table is a place of honor. Amen.

Section II: *Caring Bridge Messages*

Persistence Doesn't Always Pay Off

March 14, 2018

Thank you for coming to my Caring Bridge site to read my story of learning the diagnosis of lung cancer. It is bringing about a different plan for my future. While cancer invades my body, it doesn't change my spirit. I intend that it not change my mission in life. So, join me in the time to come and bring along a commitment to three things:

- seeing the movement of a loving God in our lives every day,

- daily laughter, and a

- tireless love for others.

I'm deeply touched that you have made this visit. My prayers include you--so in whatever the surprises of life, you'll know grace and peace and see hope abound.

After four months of a persistent cough, at times masked by a sinus infection and more often denied by a stubborn independent guy, I had a chest x-ray on February 22. The initial read suspected pneumonia. A 10-day regimen of an antibiotic followed by another x-ray was the order. On March 7 a second x-ray showed no improvements and that the cough had not changed. Persistence wasn't a good thing.

Thanks to awesome physicians (Dr. Aron Adkins, Dr. Kyle Dettbarn, Dr. Mark Hofer) I received fast moving, top-notch diagnosis and care. I was quickly evaluated and underwent a CT scan on Friday, March 9. This generated a report indicating multiple masses in the right lung.

On Monday, March 12, I underwent a bronchoscopy of the lung. On Tuesday, March 13, I learned the masses are adenocarcinoma--non-small cell cancer. That afternoon I received a referral to Mayo Clinic Health Cancer Center Eau Claire, and an appointment was scheduled with an oncologist for Thursday, March 15. How is that for fast!

Stepping back from the rapidly developing story, I am encouraged and confident. I have you, along with a myriad of loving, life-giving family and friends--a circle of love, faithfulness and hope. I have top-notch medical professionals providing care who are friends I cherish and experts I admire. I have a mother and three siblings (also cool, loving nephews and nieces and cousins) all who are foundational in my life, as well as a constant source of support and care. I have the best insurance, a Care Coordinator, and no worries about balancing work and finances during any regimen of treatment to come.

But foremost, I have the utmost trust in a God who gives life abundantly. No matter what is to come, God is ahead, above, below, behind and beside me (and you, too!). What's better than that?

A line from a favorite Easter hymn is my theme for this week: "Grant grace sufficient for life's day--that by our lives we truly say, 'Christ has triumphed! He is risen.'" *(Lutheran Book of Worship, Hymn 143).*

This afternoon, I'm looking at an ice-covered lake. The long, cold, snowy winter here on the shores of Silver Lake persists longer than last year, but I know deep within that spring is dawning. Easter is just a couple weeks away, too. I will be persistent in trusting that God in Christ will bring new life again to us all and to this world.

Thanks for reading this far! God bless you and keep you. Come again and be persistent in all things good, merciful, redemptive and life-giving.

When You Are Wondering What to Do

March 16, 2018

Yesterday, was my first opportunity to meet Dr. Al-Hattab, the oncologist from the Mayo Cancer Health Center in Eau Claire who will care for me in the effort to hold off this cancer for some time to come. He is the newest in the circle of outstanding medical professionals caring for me. Dr. Al-Hattab comes each month to Cumberland Health Care, which is only eight miles from my home.

Dr. Al-Hattab provided me a realistic, understandable, hopeful look at what possibilities are ahead in addressing the Stage 4 non-small cell lung cancer. Today I undergo in Eau Claire, a PET scan and brain MRI. The scan will show anywhere in my body where cancer cells have migrated and taken up residence. The brain MRI will show the same.

At the same time molecular testing will occur out in Seattle on the lung tissue retrieved last Monday. The aim is to determine if there is a genetic mutation at play in this cancer that would permit a newer therapy in lieu of traditional chemotherapy.

Yesterday was also a day filled with seeing and talking to people who have been part of my life for many years. I ran short of fingers and toes counting and thanking God for them in my bedtime prayers. They, along with you, are wellsprings of life and joy for me. It was truly a day full of grace.

Many people have asked what they could do for me "besides pray." I have not had a good response, but I do this morning:

- Pray that this cancer has the genetic mutation. The newer, targeted therapy would be easier and potentially allow and provide a quality of life for a longer time.

- Call that friend or family member and set up a coffee or dinner date - and enjoy laughter and companionship. You will feel better. And if you happen to be in the Rice Lake area, maybe I'll join you.

Remember this week's theme: "Grant grace sufficient for life's day."

When Winter Gives Way

March 19, 2018

The final hours of winter are upon those of us living in the northern hemisphere. Spring arrives tomorrow-- so says the calendar. My friends in Australia are saying goodbye to summer and pulling on fleece. In contrast, I am ready to pack mine away for six months or longer! The path of the sun is shifting and depending upon where you live, your perspective varies. Fall versus Spring. Warm versus cool. Dark versus light.

Truth be told, this has been the longest winter of my life. I have not felt well throughout this season of darkness. At times the bitter cold, cutting wind, and depth of snow has seemed dauntless. But next door to me, my winter-loving brother and nephew have had their best snowmobiling and ice-fishing season in years. Viewpoints vary.

As spring emerges, new perspectives dawn. My spirits always rise come spring. I look for tiny signs of life that have been unseen or unheard for many months. They start slowly, silently. Then the pace increases day by day until at some point in May around my home--life dauntlessly bursts forth everywhere and ready or not, we are caught up in the full glamour and glory of new life. We are recipients of this gift of abundant life-- nothing is asked of us.

Currently, I'm looking for tiny signs as I await the report on the molecular tests on tissues. This week is quieter in comparison to last week's dizzying pace. I will be back at

Mayo Clinic Health System Eau Claire this Friday (March 22) for a needle biopsy on some other tumor in the chest. Last week's PET scan and brain MRI indicated the need for further diagnostic work.

I continue to look for and readily find life around me and I'm grateful each day:

- For the men and women who apply their gifts, skills and passions in health care.

- For you, friends near and far who offer prayers, communication and love that bring the movement toward spring in my mind, heart and soul. Thank you!

- For awesome siblings and my mom who each day touch me with love and care.

Keep praying for the lab tests on the tissues to show the genetic mutation to allow the newer, targeted treatment. I am thinking news of that outcome by the EASTER weekend would be a wonderful addition to the grandest Good News that God brings life out of death.

This week's theme: (again from an Easter hymn)

"Oh, fill us, Lord, with *dauntless* love: Set heart and mind on things above that we conquer through your triumph." *(Lutheran Book of Worship #143).*

Mixologies of Life

March 24, 2018

Dear friends, thank you for visiting this page and for the comments. They lift my spirits and undergird my hope. The week started with no appointments permitting three days of normalcy. On Thursday I learned several things:

1. The testing on the lung tissue came back positive for one genetic mutation called PDL-1. We are still hoping for further results. Yet, this is good news, yet we await word on whether the ALK gene is the root cause of this cancer. Thanks for the prayers.

2. The above result eliminated the need for a biopsy, so I had an unplanned day off on Friday.

3. The PET scan shows significant spread of the cancer to other places, including a very small spot on the brain.

This coming Monday and Tuesday I will be at Mayo Clinic in Rochester for the Gamma Knife® procedure to address that spot. Gamma Knife is a non-invasive stereotactic radiosurgery instrument that involves no scalpel or incision. Instead it uses hundreds of precisely focused beams of radiation to control malignant brain tumors, without harming surrounding healthy tissue. How's that for cool?

Yesterday I met with Deb Hallingstad, the oncology nurse at Cumberland Healthcare where I will receive chemotherapy soon. She oriented me to the do's and don'ts ahead and shared the chemical cocktail to be served up in four hours every three weeks. The mix will include three drugs, one being Keytruda that you see advertised on television. Yes, this treatment will not be as easy as I had hoped. The goal is palliation, meaning "to relieve or lessen without curing; mitigate, alleviate." When I was a student, I never asked for an extension on an assignment. I'm asking for one now.

The news this week makes me think that everything in this life is a mix: young/old, happy/sad, exciting/boring, fast/slow, long/short, good/bad, healthy/sick. We wouldn't know one side of these pairs without the other. All of them are part of the design--the mix of life. All pose the challenge of remaining faithful, steady, focused, and hopeful.

I'm thinking Jesus was a mixologist. He said things such as *"Do not fear"* when his followers were full of fear. He said *"Believe in me"* when people had little ability to trust him. He said *"I will be with you always"* when those hearing him were confused or disbelieving. He said, *"I will come again so that where I am you will be too."*

As Holy Week begins and Christians retrace the last days of Jesus, it is a mix: excitement, anticipation, confusion, betrayal, heartbreak, love, forgiveness, anger, dying, death, burial and then … surprise, astonishment, triumph, and LIFE anew.

I have no unrealistic hopes for what is to come in the mix of my life on this earth. But I know the outcome, and I know on the way that I will continue to be the recipient of a marvelous mix of grace, joy, laughter, love, care and support. For what you, God, and a top-notch team of health care professionals are providing, I am humbly grateful. Bless you!

John 16:33 "I have told you these things, so that in me you may have peace. In this world you will have trouble. But take heart! I have overcome the world."

Marking Mercy

March 26, 2018

This is my first getaway since diagnosis 14 days ago. Tonight, I'm enjoying the comforts of a Holiday Inn Express near St Mary's Hospital in Rochester where I'll be at 5:30 a.m. tomorrow for the Gamma Knife® procedure on the small tumor on the left frontal lobe. Not a vacation, but it is raining here so I'm rather glad this isn't a vacation. It does remind me that it is spring.

Today I was privileged to meet the two radiology oncologists who will have to get up very early to get a cup of coffee down before they go to work on me. Impressive folks. By 6:30 a.m. they'll be screwing on a halo, (I never played an angel in a church pageant, so I finally get a halo) then a quick brain MRI and then the "knife" and I'll be out by 9 a.m. How slick is that? If they see any other "intruders" in my brain, they get the cut also. It is a one-stop deal ahead, and I'm in great hands. Once again. Grateful.

Each morning as I awaken, I am focused on mercy. It is an underserved gift awaiting us upon arising. You and I do nothing to get it. We don't deserve it. But it is there and given the turn in my life, I grab on to it before anything diverts my attention or energy. I try to let it inform my thoughts, words, actions and responses to people. And at the end of the day I reflect to see how that mercy has been tenaciously holding me in ways I never could have predicted or scripted. Today was one of those days.

I am reminded of Lamentations 3:22-23:
"The steadfast love of the Lord never ceases; his mercies never come to an end; they are new every morning; great is your faithfulness."

I hope tomorrow you are overwhelmed with mercy as your day starts. I will already be down the path.

This week's theme: Let the mercies move you!

When It's Good to Be Defective

March 28, 2018

Dear Friends:

I have good news to share after meeting with Dr. Al-Hattab at the Mayo Cancer Center - Eau Claire today. Because of a positive lab report on the genetic mutation, ALK (anaplastic lymphoma kinase) I will not have chemo therapy as was announced last week. Instead, I will have a targeted therapy (a pill called Alectinib). Only 4% of patients with metastatic NSCLC (non-small cell lung cancer) test positive for this defect in this gene. I am happy to be in the minority and defective on this genetic front.

Starting as soon as the pills are shipped, I will take eight per day for the foreseeable future. Released in Dec 2015, this drug has shown that 80% respond positively and live with stability for two years. Even as advanced as the tumors are in my body, located from brain to bones in the hips and everywhere in between, Alectinib is shown to shrink and even eliminate them throughout the body. It will also address any future masses in the brain. Quite the pill, isn't it?

So, my friends, I am convinced your prayers for the genetic mutation to be the avenue for a more positive outcome have made the difference. Thank you! Now, I invite your prayers for an effective response to the Alectinib. I am expecting a life lease extension (with quality throughout) and that rests on more than a pill. It rests on God, your prayers, the amazing researchers who develop targeted treatments, and an oncologist who exudes a positive stance on what he believes will work well.

No other MCHS Eau Claire patient has ever presented ALK-positive. Therefore, the outcome of this targeted treatment will be watched carefully by the team. I wish they could watch you and incorporate study of your prayers and your faithfulness as it comes to apply to the health and well-being I anticipate ahead in this journey.

I continue to know that the love, prayers, support and care of hundreds are shaping this journey. I feel them. I am deeply appreciative. I promise to honor your contributions through how I move into the future, confident, secure, hopeful and faithful.

One Knocked Down

March 29, 2018

Good morning!
After an 11-minute Gamma Knife® on the brain yesterday morning, my tumor count is finally down! Don't ask how many others there are--no one has attempted to count them. But you must start at one, right?

The morning at Mayo Clinic (Rochester) for this procedure was smooth and efficient. My early-rising sister Ronda was my chauffeur. She's always on top of a plan. I got into the hospital-issued cotton outfit, received the treatment and was back into my own clothes in less than three hours. Quite amazing. Walking out of St Mary's Hospital, I felt great! I felt even better as I went on to enjoy time with friends. Thanks to Jon Fibeger and Anne Josephson, additional chauffeurs (accompanied by Marti Hofer) who ferried me from Rochester to Eau Claire, and then to Rice Lake. It could not have been a better day.

The prayers you offered (literally many hundreds of people) lifted me and I truly believe they have made the difference on the 15-day path of the awareness of this disease so far. Yesterday was marked with good news. Today will be as well. I will meet with Dr. Al-Hattab at MCHS Eau Claire and we will discuss some better-looking treatment options than I faced last Friday. This evening I will have more to share.

So, today turn your prayers to others who live with far more concerning health concerns and with less well-being and optimism. I saw many at the Mayo Clinic that remind me I still enjoy a robust life and blessings galore.

This week's theme: Let the mercies move you!

What About Waiting?

April 3, 2018

These are days of waiting. After three weeks of tests, scans, consults and efforts to fully diagnose the non-small cell lung cancer and the genetic mutations, I look back and realize I never waited. I didn't wait for appointments. I didn't sit in waiting rooms for my name to be called. I didn't wait to learn the next steps. March blew by but forgot to take winter with it.

Now with all that over, I have been waiting, and I have not liked it. I have fussed to myself and repeatedly checked online for signs that the shipment of Alectinib (the targeted therapy) has been put on a plane bound for Cumberland, Wisconsin. Alectinib is the "magic bullet" of targeted therapy for the 4 percent of lung cancer patients who test positive for the ALK (Anaplastic Lymphoma Kinase) mutation. This mutation causes a malfunction resulting in cells reproducing wildly. My body has not waited to invite malfunction to occur in numerous places. We are going to have a little talk about that someday.

Alectinib is proven to shrink, hold back or eliminate tumors including those in the brain. For some patients studies show this treatment works for two years at which time the cancer has mutated again. While I'm waiting, I have joined an ALK Positive support group via Facebook. Already in this group I have been cheered reading of successes, as well as humbled to learn of what challenges are involved with this disease as well.

I must confess I have not waited well for the Alectinib. Since the order and insurance clearance last Thursday, at times I feel like I could have had an Uber driver get me to the specialty pharmacy in Indiana to pick it up personally.

As I wrote earlier on this site, I'm committed to seeing grace everywhere and embracing mercies delivered anew each day. But I didn't have to think about waiting in the early weeks of this life-turning development. How will I integrate grace and mercy into unwanted waiting?

Then I am taken back to church on Easter. During the wonderful worship at Bethany Lutheran, Rice Lake, I listened to Pastor Grant read the resurrection account from Mark. I thought "Imagine the wearied waiting of those who stuck with Jesus through the events of his crucifixion. Imagine those who had actually heard Jesus say repeatedly he would rise and return again." Waiting for news or action, which is either good or bad is never easy.

So, to put the full faith perspective on my little brush with "waiting" right now, we are always waiting on God, like it or not. But while we wait as Christian people--as people created in the image of God--and as people very much involved in the reality of life in this world, we have a message to claim and share with enthusiasm and joy--even in our times of waiting.

Many of you celebrated that Good News last Sunday. It is about life anew. Life that comes out of death. Life abundant. Life forever. Life for all people. There is no waiting for sharing it, embracing it and living it. Grace, mercy, and waiting. They are all swept up together and the waiting is redeemed in the realities of Easter. So, I will wait more faithfully now. But when the FedEx driver finds me tucked between the snowbanks on the shores of Silver Lake, I just may share a hug and kiss before I take the first dose. Then, the real waiting begins, doesn't it?

(I continue to be blessed richly reading journal comments and receiving cards. I wish I could reply to them all. Please know I cherish your words, care and love. God bless you for being so good to me).

Majority and Minority

April 5, 2018

Good friends and especially those of you curious about how I greeted the FedEx driver delivering the Alectinib, I am happy to report after a day delay due to the Tuesday snowstorm, it arrived in time for last evening's dose. The driver was already "hoofing it" up my hilly, snow-covered drive (he wisely chose not to drive it) by the time I got to the door. I hollered out a "thank you" and grabbed the box, eager to open it and see what this new, life-sustaining (and extending) chemical concoction looked like.

As I told you last week, there is much hope put in a pill. In addressing my advanced stage cancer, it could hold back progression, and it could shrink and eliminate tumors if I come in with the majority this time. Remember, I had to be in the 4% minority of ALK positive lung cancer patients to qualify for this targeted treatment. Majority and minority. I'll take both!

As much as I know you and I are praying for this treatment to work, I am thinking beyond the pills. A recent study published in **Cancer,** a journal of the American Cancer Society, suggests a link between religious or spiritual beliefs and better physical health reported among patients with cancer. *"In our observational study, we found people who found feelings of transcendence or meaningfulness or* *peace reported feeling the least physical problems,"* said lead author Heather Jim, PhD.

I am not worried about anything. It is part of my trust in good science, your thoughts and prayers, and a God who tells us *"Do not worry."*

Jesus said: *"Therefore I tell you, do not worry about your life, what you will eat or drink; or about your body, what you will wear. Is not life more than food, and the body more than clothes? Look at the birds of the air; they do not sow or reap or store away in barns, and yet your Heavenly Father feeds them. Are you not more valuable than they?"* (Matthew 6:25-26)

The word "worry" comes from an old English word meaning "to choke or strangle." Of course, that is exactly what worry does to your productivity and happiness. Worry turns you in on yourself or your own concern; it chokes faith and trust. Worry pushes God to the periphery of life. It is a self-defeating waste of time. And when your life turns with a diagnosis of a terminal illness, there is no reason in the world to waste time.

As I take the pills each day, I am remembering how a feeling of transcendence and trust in a God of life, along with a sense of your loving thoughts and prayers accompanying me, bring me peace. I am grateful for all these daily gifts. Thank you!

By the way, so far, so good with the pills. No side effects showing up and let's agree to keep it that way.

"So, don't worry about tomorrow. God will take care of your tomorrow too. Live one day at a time" (Matthew 6:34 LB).

When the Good is Hard to See

April 15, 2018

Psalm 118:24 *"This is the day the Lord has made; let us rejoice and be glad in it."*

Since "March Madness" entered my life, I now start the day with a quick nutritional intake, so I can take the first round of eight pills. It is part of my new normal. The pills are in the family of new cancer fighting drugs which take direct aim at the foreign invaders and hold back for a time further progression of tumors.

As this mid-April day unfolds, there seems to be another foreign invader holding back the progression to spring. It is motivating many to complain. It is tamping back our mental expectations. It makes us cranky and ungrateful. Spirits sag as spring is pushed further into the future.

One thing I am learning in this new normal life is to keep perspective on the things I can and cannot manage. I cannot manage how this drug will work against a formidable disease. I can manage how I live with it. I cannot manage the effectiveness of the drug to knock back the tumors. I can manage my thoughts and attitudes and perspectives. I cannot stop the snow from falling. I can anticipate with joy the season to come.

So, on that note, I think about that verse at the top of this page. If each day is a gift from God, then I must look for the goodness in it. I can choose to see its beauty, or I can complain about what it does or doesn't contain.

On the March day I was diagnosed with lung cancer, I wasn't given a choice. But it was a day God had given me and one in which there was reason to rejoice. There have been amazing, compassionate medical people telling me about options and next steps. There are loving family and friends beside me. The sun was shining and there was a smell of spring in the air. *"Let us rejoice and be glad in it."*

There are days in our lives when it is difficult to see the beauty--the reasons to *"rejoice and be glad."* But God is not stopped by our limitations or our perspectives. The gift of each day has its own efficacy. And, isn't that in itself a reason to be glad!

So, if you have eyes of faith to see, you will realize there is reason to rejoice and be glad even when life turns abruptly--or the snow is deep in mid-April.

When Something Ordinary Became a Revelation

April 22, 2018

Living with advanced lung cancer is teaching me new things. Most of them are not revelations. Many of these lessons are ordinary at face value. They are adjustments regarding what I do and don't eat and drink to best serve the drug prescribed to knock back the tumors. It includes taking all the vitamin supplements to build up defenses and boost immunity. Many of the new things revolve around managing the best approach to this disease. Ultimately, the aim is to enjoy no progression of the cancer for as long as possible.

But this morning at worship something ordinary became a revelation. It was not anything new at face value. It happened at the start of worship when I realized I could sing again! For the first time in six months I could add my voice to those around me as the good people of Bethany offered praises to God led by outstanding teen and adult musicians. I could once again sing with them:

Now the feast and celebration, all of creation sings for joy.

After a painfully long winter, I was once again part of the creation singing for joy. Thanks to an amazingly fast-acting, effective targeted treatment named Alectinib, I am no longer coughing. Gone are the catches down deep in my right lung. Gone is the pain stopping me from trying to sing. This morning there was no more lip-syncing and passively watching the words on the screen, feeling like a spectator versus a participant. Today my body had the ability and strength to get caught up in singing as I have done for years with resultant joy.

There are some things that have been permanently lost to me because of this disease. I'm learning to live with them as part of the adjustments under way. But today I was reminded that some things cannot be lost because they reside deep in our souls; but more importantly, in the heart of God.

Before that song of praise ended this morning, we sang these words: *"For God has come to dwell with us, to make us people of God, to make all things new."*

Do you see the grace in the subject and in the object of that sentence? It is the heart of God to be with us and to claim us. That is a soul-warming grace. But it gets better. Considering a terminal cancer diagnosis bringing weighty new realities to life, the soaring good news is that this God makes all things new and that grace has the power to lift the soul, no matter one's weighty circumstances.

So, I ask myself: "What am I to do with this gift?" For me, at least today, when I realized that the treatment is working, and a cough no longer stops my singing impulses, I just sang. Sang with joy. Sang with thanksgiving. I made my lung sing right on by all the tumors.

Then I remembered this verse: *What am I to do? I will pray with my spirit, but I will pray with my mind also; I will sing praise with my spirit, but I will sing with my mind also. 1 Corinthians 14:15.*

Thank you for your prayers and the warm notes of care and love. You bless my spirit and my mind. For now, I continue to improve. My blood levels are holding up. Energy inches up, while fatigue holds on, likely a side effect of the drug. I am looking forward to advancing my new normal life this summer. Meanwhile, I hope that this summer will bring the FDA approval of the next generation of targeted treatment for ALK positive lung cancer patients. This could mean that when Alectinib no longer works for me, because the cancer has mutated again, I could be a beneficiary of this new drug.

And the reasons to sing will continue! This week, I hope you will sing with all the voices of your spirit and mind.

At A Minimum

April 26, 2018

Isn't it true that we tend to look at unplanned or unwanted major life changes with an eye to what has been lost? What changes in our outlook and attitude if we, at the minimum, keep an eye on what has not been lost? I think this poem helps those of us living with cancer. Maybe for us all there is a new perspective here, too.

Cancer is so limited
It cannot cripple love
It cannot shatter hope
It cannot corral faith
It cannot eat away peace
It cannot kill friendship
It cannot shut out memories
It cannot silence courage
It cannot invade the soul
It cannot reduce eternal life
It cannot quench the spirit
It cannot lessen the power of resurrection[6]

---

[6] https://csn.cancer.org/node/174893

Marathon Musings

May 6, 2018

Today was an awesome day! It was the 10th annual Eau Claire Marathon and for the first time, I was free on a Sunday morning to see this event from its central hub at Carson Park. What a fabulous event. It drew a record 4700 participants.

Under the outstanding direction of Pat Toutant and his daughter Emily Uelmen, runners tell me this is becoming a favorite spring marathon in this part of the country. They like the precision of the course and the beauty it provides. I am told they also appreciate the community support seen in 800 volunteers and an estimated 25,000 spectators cheering on runners, walkers and wheelers.

I was at the marathon today because Pat invited me to provide the blessing of participants at the three starting times. It was an honor and a pleasure to have a tiny role inspiring those setting out to do something that, even if I wanted to, I could not physically do because of this disease.

At each start, determination and strength was on the faces of the runners. As they crossed the starting line I cheered and watched as they disappeared down the road, relaying the cheers and shouts of spectators lining the course out of my sight.

Life is a marathon for each of us. Sometimes we attempt to sprint parts of it, hurrying to achieve a goal or run away from a challenge. At times we get weary and try to sit out life's pressure or disappointments. Other times we look for someone else to run parts for us or provide us a ride to a better point. But life doesn't offer us any options but to run the marathon.

Living with stage 4 cancer is part of my marathon I never dreamed would appear on the course. But today, the runners and cheering crowds reminded me of two things:

1. Face the course with determination.

2. Look for and find strength that comes from outside yourself.

I am strengthened by your cheers of care, concern, compassion and love. All of you point me to God who has promised to continually renew our strength of the living of this life.

Isaiah 40:28-31 "Have you not known? Have you not heard? The Lord is the everlasting God, the Creator of the ends of the earth. He does not faint or grow weary; his understanding is unsearchable. He gives power to the faint and strengthens the powerless. Even youths will faint and be weary, and the young will fall exhausted; but those who wait for the Lord shall renew their strength, they shall mount up with wings like eagles, they shall run and not be weary, they shall walk and not faint."

For all who greeted me today and for reunions with friends, thank you! You put a face on the great crowd that is cheering me through this challenge. Thanks Pat, Kerry, Em and all the Toutant family for the kind hospitality today as well.

This past week my fabulous medical team infused me with a drug called Zometa. In my case it is a support drug to treat symptoms and decrease complications (such as fractures or pain) produced by bone metastasis. I have full trust it will strengthen me for this marathon. But for a couple of days it cranked on me with pain I had not previously encountered. I am fine now, so no need to worry or feel sorry for me. Yet, please keep on cheering in whatever way you choose: prayer, good thoughts, greetings or visits. The strength you provide is amazing and every muscle and bone in me is grateful. You bless this "new normal" life I'm pursuing.

Here's the blessing I shared this morning:
Gracious Creator, thank you for the gift of this day and this event in our beautiful city. Bless all these runners, walkers and wheelers as they course throughout this city. Keep them safe. Inspire their pursuits – whether they set out to achieve personal goals, support an organization or run in honor or memory of someone special. Give them strength, courage and motivation to press on toward their goal.

Thank you for all who make this race possible: race directors and organizers, police officers, medical professionals, community volunteers, sponsors and the 25,000 spectators who cheer them on to the finish.

At the end of this marathon and at the end of this day, may we look back with gratitude for the goodness that has accompanied us, the goals achieved, and the love that supports us all for living fully, today, every day and always.

New Normal to Live

May 19, 2018

Good morning dear friends,

This will be a quick post. I promise more will follow shortly.

It has been nearly two weeks since I have posted an update. The worn phrase "no news is good news" does apply to the quiet of recent weeks. The pain of Zometa left after a week. I have learned that the pain was a sign of the good work it aims to provide.

So, with better days, I have been diligent doing the things that are good for me, per my outstanding oncology nurse Deb Hallingstad: drinking copious amounts of water, taking in lots of protein, taking the Alectinib every 12 hours, and interspersing supplements for things like bone and nervous system well-being.

I have also been enjoying activities that occupy mind and body. Gentle exercise is good they tell me, so my bones don't "bark." To that end I have enjoyed longer walks to test endurance (with new, fancy sticks thanks to the tips from Steve Endres and Todd Wright) and revamping part of my perennial garden. Spring is almost given fully to summer on the shores of Silver Lake. Life is brimming with goodness around and within. I am grateful.

As I write I am enjoying my first foray away from Wisconsin since diagnosis. Dr Al-Hattab approved, at the start of this treatment, that travel was permissible and "normal" life should be embraced. Yes, please laugh. You know my normal which often seems anything but normal. And cancer does bring a very, very different understanding of normal.

I have an oncology update to share which I received just before leaving Wisconsin two days ago. Crafting it takes some time and I am cogitating and have not had time to accomplish it. So please check back this evening for more. For now, I am off to seek out some breakfast (with protein!) and then a morning walk to pursue. "Normal" life to live. I will be back soon.

Meanwhile, thank you for checking in, for prayers and positive thoughts, and for the life you embrace with gratitude and share in abundance.

The Miracle for Now

May 19, 2018

As promised, I have an oncology update from May 17 to share. Thanks for coming back to learn the news. It is good. No, it is incredible! It is a stunner, shaking off the shock of seeing a scan of my body back in March that showed a lung full of tumors large and small. If that wasn't enough, it showed tumors dotting in such places as liver, kidneys, bones and brain.

A chest X-ray on May 16 aimed to give us a quick, inexpensive look at what Alectinib has been doing in the lung after six weeks. A larger scope scan will follow in six weeks.

I read that Alectinib (the targeted therapy) has been reported to have potent efficacy in ALK-positive lung cancer patients. This X-ray shows that my case adds to the report.

On Thursday, an enthusiastic Dr. Al-Hattab of the Mayo Cancer Center in Eau Claire reported that he sees on the X-ray of the lung no sign of any tumors. You read that right. I heard it right and I blinked. He smiled. Then he said, "This gives me chills."

Gone. "Shot out." Blown away are the uninvited cellular intruders who gave me a cough for months. A miracle for now! A product of extraordinary science all wrapped up in a pill! A gift of a wise, skilled, up-to-date oncologist. I see this as:

- An outcome of your prayers;

- A combination of the power of faith bringing such a vast community together to cheer for me and bring about positive outcomes.

Many words come to mind: amazing; unexpected; appreciation; awe-inspiring.

Since this life turn in March, I've never asked "why me." Some of you have noted the unfairness of this reality. I have not asked God any pointed questions of "why" or "how come." It doesn't really interest me to know, though I respect those who do wonder. Rather, I am more intent on living now and for the future.

I noted "miracle for now" above. Cancer is elusive and persistent. There will be tumor-laden challenges another day. But today! Today's report is a gift for inspiring life now. It raises my spirits and like the good, mysterious, elusive and effective Holy Spirit, it provides a miracle that is only worth something as it takes hold of us and moves. It is a miracle that must be extended for the sake of others and the world.

Tomorrow many of you will worship as the Christian church celebrates Pentecost-- the third major festival marking the biblical account of the Spirit coming upon people.

As I think about the Holy Spirit anew this spring, I realize the Spirit is about so much more than miracles in life. As you will hear tomorrow, the Spirit does not remove challenges and hardships from Jesus' followers, but rather equips them to persevere, even flourish, amid them.

In the Gospel of John, the disciples are hiding in a room out of fear that those who crucified Jesus may come after them. And what does Jesus do as he breathes on them the Holy Spirit? He does not take them away from danger or fortify the room in which they are hiding. Instead, he sends them out into that dangerous world (20:21), and then He gives them the gift of the Holy Spirit to create in them the courage they will need to follow Jesus' command. A miracle of faith!

Later, the Spirit is given to enable people to look beyond their individual needs, hopes, or fears and equip them with distinct gifts, all in order to work together for the "common good" (1 Corinthians 12:7).

I don't believe the Spirit is a super hero sent to rescue us; but rather the one who equips, encourages, and stays with us, helping us perceive the needs of our neighbors and community and then rise to the occasion to meet those needs with equal measures of tenacity, competence, and courage.

We often hope that the Spirit will just plain save us, or at least to take us away from whatever challenges seems to threaten to overwhelm us in the moment. But the operation of the Spirit seems to be "with" rather than "from" --as in being "with us" during challenges rather than "taking those challenges away from us."

For now, the immediate challenge of freeing a tumor infested lung has been accomplished. I know the Spirit was with me and my faithful, appointment attending sister Ronda, and Dr. Al-Hattab and nurse Debb in that little room in Cumberland hospital on Thursday. It was the miracle of tumor destruction in this important organ. The miracle of another life extension didn't just happen willy-nilly. It was something so much greater!

So, what does the Spirit do and how do miracles go beyond surprising us and granting us the impossible or improbable? That is the real question, isn't it?

I recognize that while we may often hope that God will remove us from challenging or difficult situations, God instead comes along side us in the presence of the Holy Spirit in order to strengthen and equip us to endure, and even to flourish, amid these challenges and difficulties. Why? Perhaps because God may be working miracles through us for the common good to care for the needs of our neighbors, community, and world.

We have a purpose no matter what challenges exist in our lives:

- to care for those around us as God cares for us;

- to make wherever we may find ourselves a better place;

- to share God's love in word and deed that all people may know they are not alone and, indeed loved.

We are here, which is a miracle, and that is, not simply for ourselves.

The Promise of God's Spirit is not that we will suffer no more difficulty or hardships, nor that God will remove us from challenges. Rather than in the Holy Spirit, God comes to be with us, and be for us, and to use all that we have and are for the sake of those around us. It is an incredible promise, when you think of it, and it is a miracle of the highest which deserves to be shared once again.

So, thank you dear friends, for your part in the "Miracle for Now." Meanwhile, I will keep on popping eight pills a day, living the new normal, and sharing the miracle we all have to enjoy, steward, and share.

Living with Cancer is Like Mastering Golf

May 31, 2018

My friends, since I last wrote to you with the good news of a lung unburdened of tumors, I have no medical update to share. In three weeks more extensive scans will provide a keen look from brain to hips to see how other tumors have fared against the magic bullet, the targeted treatment called Alectinib.

In these ordinary-seeming days, while I am feeling good, I am pondering what it means and how it works to live well with cancer.

Best I can figure, it's like playing golf. You can know all the fundamentals, but the mental part is what will make or break your game. Same with this deal I am striving to learn. I have the fundamentals in place, thanks to amazing medical care and an effective treatment regimen. Yet the mental part is the challenge. It is hard to know what is possible when you have a terminal cancer. Even when it is being well-controlled via drugs and life seems normal, you still have an incurable disease.

So, it is hard to know what is possible. How does one think about making plans or dreaming about goals in the same way others do who do not have such a diagnosis? What's realistic to anticipate in six or twelve months? If I make plans further out, will I still feel good enough to complete them?

When you have cancer, some expect you to look sick. When you do not show illness, they go to the other end of the spectrum and think you are healthy; when the truth is it is a combination of both. Prior to a recent appointment I had to complete a questionnaire and check "Poor" for my health status, when for years I proudly checked "Excellent." How did that happen? Shifting the mind is a daunting effort.

So, there has been a switch up in the mental game of life. I liken it to golf where when I tried the game, I wanted to drive the ball down the fairway, but it rarely went where I wanted it to go. I could never get into the mental aspect of the game. My dad provided lessons as a kid. I took lessons as an adult. But I always had a mental block that I couldn't conquer so I could have any chance of enjoy golfing.

Now, I have a much harder game to play and I cannot let a mental block stop me from achieving "par" every day. There just isn't time to waste! I am told the median PFS (progression free survival) for patients with central nervous system involvement taking Alectinib is 27 months. That isn't a long span when I realize I'm only weeks away from having been retired two years. Time does fly!

Short of trying golf lessons again and applying them to this endeavor of learning to live well with cancer, I guess I'm going to have to try another approach.

Now, you know I am a preacher and you have heard the jokes that we preachers have a "direct line" or we are "closer to the Big Guy." Thus, challenges should be more easily solved or conquered. But this incurable disease, while it seems to be headed to the weeds off the fairway for a while, remains a formidable challenge to one's mental well-being.

But that is when I realize I must go back to the fundamentals that have been firmly in place for all my life. It is the only hope to live well, given this challenge.

Jesus reminded challenged people such as me that faith is like a mustard seed. One day the disciples said to Jesus, *"Increase our faith!" He replied, "If you have faith as small as a mustard seed, you can say to this mulberry tree, 'Be uprooted and planted in the sea,' and it will obey you.'" (Luke 15)*

The disciples want Jesus to give them more faith to face their challenges. Yet as Jesus explains it, faith isn't quantifiable, and it isn't an idea. It is not simply a mental thing. It is a muscle. It needs to be moved. And the more we use that muscle, the stronger it gets.

So, Jesus is telling me, as he told those disciples long ago, that I have what I need to overcome the mental challenge that came in a diagnosis 2 ½ months ago. Use faith to overcome any mental challenge by being about:

- doing our work

- raising our children and grandchildren

- reaching out to the lonely and grieving

- caring for and befriending others

- contributing to the common good.

This is how we overcome mental challenges, exercising everyday faith, no matter what.

So, as I practice living well with cancer, don't look to see me carting the sticks around the links. That's a mental challenge I won't take a swing at. However, I would join you for a walk along the fairway.

When's Mercy's Specialty Brings a Miracle

June 23, 2018

Dear Friends,

As the full beauty of summer in Wisconsin envelops and the sunlight reaches its longest span in this part of the world, I'm happy to contribute a big beam of good news to all who have been partners in prayer and eager watchers of news regarding my health. Since the blustering snowstorms of March and April and the diagnosing of lung cancer, much has transpired.

Yesterday I was at the Mayo Cancer Center in Eau Claire for my first quarterly evaluation. A PET scan and brain MRI reveals that, after 11 weeks on Alectinib (the targeted treatment specific to the ALK-positive type lung cancer I have), the cancer has been pushed into remission. All the tumors in the lung and those from brain to hips do not appear on the scan. "Complete remission" Dr. Al-Hattab said through his smile as he pointed at the monitor showing the miracle. He wasn't surprised. I was.

It is a miracle of good science and a sign of the incredible advances being made in genomic research and treatment of many types of cancer. I am the recipient of the investments of uncounted people, knowledge, dedication, investment and experimentation that has led to all the medical care I have been given in three months. The results speak for themselves, don't they?

There is also a miracle in addition to and in cooperation with the medical. It is one I know you're not overlooking or dismissing. Why? Because you've invested in caring, praying and forming a network that has transforming power.

There is a guy named Hezekiah, a king, who appears in the Old Testament book of Isaiah. Hezekiah (don't you love the name?) was seriously ill and the prophet Isaiah came to him and told him to prepare himself for his death. We are told Hezekiah, in tears, turned his face to the wall and prayed to the Lord saying, 'Please, remember how I have walked before you in faithfulness and with a whole heart, and have done what is good in your sight.'"

Hezekiah doesn't get a direct response, but rather one that comes through the prophet Isaiah. *"Then the word of the Lord came to Isaiah: 'Go and say to Hezekiah, Thus says the Lord...I have heard your prayer; I have seen your tears...This shall be the sign to you...the Lord will do this thing that he has promised: Behold, I will make the shadow cast by the declining sun on the dial of Ahaz turn back ten steps.' So, the sun turned back..." (Isaiah 38:2-8).* Hezekiah lived 15 more years.

Hezekiah seemed to know God is merciful and that is what got God's attention. Hezekiah didn't try to negotiate with

God. Instead of bargaining or arguing, he just asked for mercy. Mercy is God's specialty. Hezekiah prayed. He didn't blame, curse or deny God. He prayed immediately, intensely. I want to think that Hezekiah had his friends and family praying, too.

So, how does God reveal a response? God reveals the gift of an extension of life to Hezekiah in a dramatic fashion: *"I will make the shadow cast by the sun go back the ten steps..."* Realize for this sign to take place, the earth had to move backwards in its spin. This is potentially a global cataclysmic event with potential tidal waves and earthquakes. Whether literally or metaphorically, God turned the world on its axis to show faithfulness to Hezekiah and the people he ruled. Notice the result: circumstances and destinies were changed.

For now, and once again, my circumstances have changed, and it will take some time to figure out a few things. A bit of my world has shifted yet again. But beyond the miracle of yesterday, I realize something more lasting and overarching. Prayer is our best first move, not our last resort. Prayer changes us and our circumstances. God wants us to pray and God delights in the relationship that can be changed because we pray. Indeed, God answers prayer through others, too.

Oh, yes, I believe that God supplies our needs even when we don't pray. But failing to pray deprives us of opportunities to see God's presence in our lives and the relationships that are changed because of prayer.

My friends, thank you for showing me God's presence through your prayers over the past three months - the cards and kind deeds, too. Maybe now is a good time to take up a new prayer cause - for someone else, for a relationship, for our society, for our churches, for the very world. For I hope you see in a renewed way, the power of prayer and a God who mercifully acts in direct response.

For now, I will continue to take Alectinib, eight pills a day and hope that I reach or surpass the evidential median of 27 months before the cancer mutates and progresses. The unwanted invaders aren't gone. This is not a cure. This cancer will come back with a different genomic mix so that the Alectinib won't work anymore. Then there will be Lorlatinib or another new drug to try in order to keep extending this miracle.

What won't change is the power of prayer and even better, the mercy which is God's specialty. There's nothing else needed, is there? So, press on my friends, living your amazing life with faithfulness and servanthood. I will be back in touch another day.

Interventions of Hope

On November 8, 2018 I was a guest of the Mayo Clinic Health System at a fund-raising dinner in Eau Claire called "Hope for the Valley." The room was filled with nearly 300 people who have been touched and changed by cancer and yet they remain grateful and hopeful. Below is my address.

Good evening,

Tonight, for the first time I tell my story to a group of folks that I don't know, but folks with whom I sense a bond. You are here because you care about people living with cancer. You make life better for people whose lives have been changed by cancer.

Thank you for your presence this evening. Thank you to Mayo Clinic Health System for inviting me and providing an opportunity to share a few words.

"Cancer"! In the space of time it takes to utter the word, it has the power to upend your way of life and your peace of mind.

Eight months ago, I was told I have non-small cell lung cancer, stage 4 with mets in the brain and spine, in bones and around many major organs.

I have lived a healthy life. I have never been a smoker. We lung cancer patients feel the need to add that information, lest anyone think we engaged in behaviors that led to our cancer. Year after year my primary physician, whom I respect and appreciate enormously, would smile at the conclusion of my annual physical and proclaim me very healthy. I could expect to live a very long life, he would add.

On March 9 when I was told of this diagnosis, a seismic intervention occurred. Everything seemed to change. That makes it sound like everything changed for the worse, though, doesn't it? That is not true. Much did not change. And some changes have been very positive.

At the start, life was a blur of consultations, scans, and a fascinating procedure at the Mayo Clinic to "zap" a small tumor in the brain. Calls and texts with offers of help came from hundreds of people.

I said a moment ago that a seismic intervention occurred when I first heard the word cancer. The word "intervene" means "to come between so as to prevent or modify an outcome." As I think back over eight months of living with cancer, I have been the beneficiary of untold interventions of hope.

Hope is our most vital asset – the most needed virtue of our time. When people ask me how I stay hopeful while living with this disease, I tell them "Hope keeps cancer from defining my life and taking control of daily living."

But try as hard as I can, I can't build up hope on my own. I can't train for hope like I would train to run a marathon. No, hope comes from beyond us and when cancer intervenes in our lives, we need people who intervene with hope. In the past 8 months there have been many.

Dr. Al-Hattab, my Mayo Cancer Center oncologist gives me hope. His sober response to my diagnosis did not dent his confidence that he could treat me successfully, so as to expect two years of progression free survival on a new drug called Alectinib. There are others who intervene with hope. Debbie Hallingstad, nurse alongside Dr. Al-Hattab at Cumberland Healthcare is steadfast in providing for me, offering herself 24/7. My family, my 3 siblings here this evening and a huge circle of friends have intervened with hope through word and deed. I also think of people I will never meet, researchers and scientists developing genetic testing for cancers and those who develop new, amazing therapies to go after those genetic mutations … they intervene with hope. There are patients who agree to be part of trials so new drugs can be tested. They give their very lives to intervene with hope.

But tonight, I think of you intervening with hope through your support of Hope in the Valley. Hundreds of people will benefit because of your generosity and caring.

One last word. In June I was declared to be in remission. Up to that point, I didn't know that word ever applied to stage 4 lung cancer. Another intervention of hope.

I expect many more interventions ahead as I move into an increasingly challenging future. The reality is we all have daily opportunities to be people of hope. Thank you for intervening with hope this evening.

Gratitude

November 21, 2018

This Thanksgiving holiday seems like the right time to post an update. Unlike previous posts, this one is not prompted by a change in health. The adage "No news is good news" has applied since late June. I continue to benefit from amazing treatment, world-class medical care, excellent insurance, your prayers and well-wishes. Thank you.

This holiday I am thankful, but that seems a bit thin this year. The truth is I am deeply grateful and gratitude is richer, wider, and enduring. Gratitude is a feeling and action, it's personal and communal. Gratitude is inherently social for it connects us. Thankfulness seems more transactional to me. This holiday we say we're thankful for health, healing, family, friends, economic well-being, and so on. But gratitude is not about an exchange. It's always about free gifts and grace.

Before the end of the year I will have a PET scan and brain MRI again to measure the success of the ongoing daily treatment in holding the ALK positive mutation in check. That mutation caused the lung cancer. Dr. Al-Hattab believes this drug will work for two years and so far, nine months in, the results are encouraging, so far miraculous. (*see link below for story)

This Thanksgiving I'm reflecting on the fruits of gratitude and many interventions of hope that have marked an extraordinary span of time. Your involvement and regard have helped me see the gifts and grace of gratitude and feel the buoyancy of hope.

So, thank you dear Caring Bridge friends and best wishes for a rich and delightful, grateful Thanksgiving.

Notes

Mayo Clinic Hometown Health published a story on my case called "Modern Miracle: Advances in treatment keep cancer in check.

See it at:

https://mayoclinichealthsystem.org/hometown-health/patient-stories/modern-miracle-treatment-advances

The Nature of Living in the Now

January 1, 2019

Good friends via Caring Bridge--it's a new year and I have good news. Just before Christmas my latest PET scan and brain MRI show that the targeted treatment continues to hold back the cancer. There are no new spots! In 6 months, barring any new symptoms arising sooner, this regimen will be repeated.

Since last March when I first learned lung cancer had metastasized to several primary organs and into the bones and brain, I resolved to live more gratefully each day. It seemed the only suitable response to my forced awareness of the miracle of being alive in the first place. I am not always successful at this mindful living, however. For inspiration I look to my dog, Elle, who lives constantly in the here and now. Of course, I look to God, too! You expected me to say that, right? You inspire me, too!

2018 reminded me in a new, more personal way, of the beauty and fragility of life. It also makes me wonder if this becomes more evident to those who live with a terminal diagnosis? I think the answer is yes.

Occasionally, pop culture comes up with a way to reveal the nature of living in the now. In "Groundhog Day," Bill Murray's character must repeat the same day over and over. His redemption story concludes with Murray evolved into a wise man, capable of love, delivering this epiphany: "No matter what happened before or happens after, I'm happy now."

I figure the best I can do, regardless of the world's uncertainties big and small, is emulate that attitude. No matter how grateful I am to a targeted therapy for the chance to live longer, I am determined not to take another moment on time's continuum for granted. As an extension, I've promised myself to make some positive contribution to the future every day and that has brought some notable delights.

As I think of 2019 and coming to the first anniversary of this diagnosis and the start of the second of the two years my oncologist hopes I get out of the current treatment, I know there will be joy and beauty no matter what happened before or happens after. I will recognize the experience for what it is — a gift of bonus time, an argument for being grateful and happy now.

Wishing you and yours the delights of making a difference in this world every day. Thanks for reading my post.

Bibliography

All Biblical quotations are from *The New Revised Standard Version,* copyright 1989, 1995 by the Division of Christian Education of the National Council of Churches of Christ in the United States of America. Used by permission. All rights reserved.